D0874012

Southeast Florida Pioneers
The Palm and Treasure Coasts

William E. McGoun

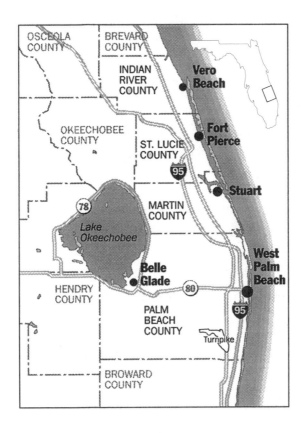

Pineapple Press, Inc.

Sarasota, Florida

Inquiries should be addressed to:
Pineapple Press, Inc.
P.O. Box 3899
Sarasota, Florida 34230

Library of Congress Cataloging in Publication Data

McGoun, William E., 1937–
    Southeast Florida pioneers : the palm and treasure coasts / by
    William E. McGoun. — 1st ed.
        p.   cm.
    Includes bibliographical references and index.
    ISBN 1-56164-157-X (alk. paper)
    1. Palm Beach County (Fla.)—History. 2. Frontier and pioneer life—
Florida—Palm Beach County. 3. Pioneers—Florida—Palm Beach
County—Biography. 4. Palm Beach County (Fla.)—Biography.
I. Title.
F317.P2M38   1998
975.9'32—dc21   98-20285
                        CIP

First Edition
10 9 8 7 6 5 4 3 2 1

Design by Sandra Wright's Designs
Printed and bound by Edwards Brothers, Inc., Lillington, North Carolina

Contents

Introduction

It is often said that South Florida has no history, but that isn't so. It would be more accurate to say that South Floridians have no sense of the area's history. After all, most of us were born elsewhere, and many have come south only upon retirement. I myself was born in Pennsylvania, though I am somewhat of an honorary native because I came to Lake Worth when I was six.

South Florida actually has a rich history, even though the area's modern era only dates from the construction of Henry Flagler's Florida East Coast Railway in the 1890s. Big-game hunters were present here as many as ten thousand years ago, and well-developed Indian societies confronted the first Europeans in the sixteenth century, long before the establishment in Virginia of the first English-speaking colony in North America.

I think everyone has to age a bit before appreciating history. I know I did. I didn't get involved in writing history until 1971, at the age of thirty-three. As a child in the 1940s and 1950s, my thoughts were of the present and future. I knew that a high-school classmate was the granddaughter of Andrew Garnett, one of the original "Barefoot Mailmen," but that didn't mean anything at the time.

I have tried to create a book that is accessible to such a newcomer but still informative for the old-timer, one that has value to the academic and appeal to the layman. To make it more readable than many historical accounts, I have intertwined historical trends and the biographies of famous and not-so-famous persons. If this makes the book too episodic at times, I apologize. I have made the index as thorough as possible to compensate for any lack of organization.

The persons represented in this history range from a seventeenth-century Quaker merchant to a twentieth-century billionaire. Flagler was perhaps the most famous person in Florida history, whereas the names of many of the victims of the 1928 hurricane, buried in mass graves, will be forever unknown. Some characters, such as architect Addison Mizner and writer Zora Neale Hurston, have known national fame; others, like Marian Newhall and Arthur Glenn McKee, are hardly known today even in the towns where they lived.

I had planned to provide footnotes but changed my mind. In many cases, a statement in the book represents a compilation from a number of sources. Other times, it is a conclusion of mine or an observation based on my fifty years in South Florida. Thus, I have elected instead to put a note listing the sources at the end of each chapter. All published sources are listed in the bibliography; names of persons interviewed and libraries at which clip files were examined are in the chapter notes.

I could not have written this book without the cooperation of *The Palm Beach Post*. Among other things, *The Post* paid me for almost all of the research. With the exception of the article about the Fanjul empire, all of the chapters first appeared in some form in *The Post*. The newspaper's archives also provided most of the photographs.

Chapter 1
Jonathan Dickinson
Faith in Wilderness

The barkentine *Reformation*, in the teeth of a nor'easter while en route from Jamaica to Philadelphia, tried to beat its way northward close to the shore. The best efforts of the crew of nine were in vain, however, and the three-master was forced ashore about five miles north of Jupiter Inlet, or what then was called the mouth of Rio Jobe. The ship at first touched lightly and remained afloat. Minutes later, a surge drove it aground. It was 1 A.M. on September 24, 1696.

"The wind was violent and it was very dark, that our mariners could see no land; the seas broke over us that we were in a quarter of an hour floating in the cabin: we endeavored to get a candle lighted, which in a little time was accomplished. . . . The seas continued breaking over us and no land to be seen; we concluded to keep in the vessel as long as she would hold together," later wrote Jonathan Dickinson, the man who had hired the *Reformation*.

By morning, the seas had begun to recede, and daylight found the ship's complement "upon the shore, on a beach lying in the breach of the sea which at times as the surges of the sea reversed was dry." The ship was intact, but she was sorely damaged. Those aboard decided to abandon her before another storm caused her to collapse around them. "The wilderness country," Dickinson wrote, "looked very dismal, having no trees, but only sand hills covered with shrubby palmetto, the stalks of which were prickly, that there was no walking amongst them. I espied a place almost a furlong within that beach being a bottom. . . . We got to the place under the shelter of some few bushes which broke some of the wind, but kept none of the rain from [us]; I got a fire made."

As shipwreck victims go, those aboard the *Reformation* were fortunate indeed. No one had been killed or even seriously injured. Even the hogs and sheep aboard had made it through safely, though some hens had drowned. Dickinson, a devout Quaker, had little trouble explaining his company's good fortune: It was divine Providence. Dickinson's account of that night and the survivors' ensuing journey, which would become a best-seller on both sides of the Atlantic, contains phrases such as "blessed be the name of the Lord in Whom we trust," "except it should please the Almighty God to work wonderfully for our deliverance," and "but it pleased God to tender the hearts of some of them." And the preface to the first edition of his journal, presumably written by another Quaker, is three thousand words of continual praise to the Lord. But beyond this spiritual tribute, Dickinson's tale provides one of the best descriptions of mainland East Coast Indians during the first Spanish period in Florida (1565–1763).

Dickinson was born in Jamaica in 1663, one of seven children of Francis and Margaret Dickinson. Upon adulthood, he joined his father—a prosperous merchant and planter—in business before later deciding to establish a branch in Philadelphia (possibly as a result of the 1692 earthquake that devastated Port Royal, then the capital of Jamaica). He was able to take a cargo valued at fifteen hundred

pounds sterling, along with a company totaling twenty-five, when the *Reformation* sailed from Port Royal on August 23, 1696. Among the passengers were Dickinson, his wife, Mary Gale, and their five-month-old son, Jonathan Jr.; a well-known Quaker missionary named Robert Barrow; a Dickinson kinsman—not otherwise identified—named Benjamin Allen; eleven slaves, ten of whom were African and the eleventh, Indian; and ship's master Joseph Kirle and his crew.

The *Reformation* had been part of a convoy, as England and France were at war, but days of calm and an adverse current had caused her to drift from the other ships. Kirle sought to put his ship in at Havana (Spain and England

John R. Reis, amateur historian, costumed as Jonathan Dickinson for the 300th anniversary of Dickinson's 1696 shipwreck. There is no known picture of Dickinson. (The Palm Beach Post)

were at peace) on September 18 when a sudden squall struck from landward. The wind whipped a boom across the deck, knocking Kirle down and breaking his leg. The same afternoon, the Indian slave—a girl named Venus—had convulsions and died. The wind was favorable for northward sailing the next day, so Kirle gave up trying to reach Havana and headed toward Florida. As was and still is the custom when under sail, he kept his ship in the Gulf Stream to take advantage of a northern flow that can reach five miles per hour. But this meant the *Reformation* was too close to shore in the Jupiter area to be maneuvered when the nor'easter struck days later.

Full light found the survivors, and a considerable amount of goods they had rescued from the ship, alone on an unknown shore. They wouldn't be alone for long. "About the eighth or ninth hour came two Indian men (being naked except for a small piece of plat-ted work of straws which just hid their private parts and fastened behind with a horsetail in likeness made of a sort of silk-grass) from the southward." The Indians grabbed the first two members of the ship's party they came upon and acted as though they might kill them. Dickinson, rejecting advice that the party arm itself, went to talk with the two and gave them tobacco and pipes, "which they greedily snatched from me . . . turned their backs upon us and ran away." About noon, the Indians were back "in a great number all running and shouting." Some began looting the ship, while others, including the chief—called by Dickinson the "casseekey," probably a corruption of the Spanish *cacique*—approached the survivors and menaced them.

The Indians obviously had had contact with Spaniards. Most car-ried Spanish knives, and they seemed to like Spaniards. Englishmen were a different matter; the Indians repeatedly yelled, "Nickaleer, Nickaleer," which Dickinson finally deduced was their pronuncia-tion of "Englishman," and seized the survivors from behind as if to slit their throats. Then the Indians changed their minds, probably due largely to the efforts of sailor Solomon Cressen, who spoke Spanish fluently and convinced the Indians that the survivors were Spanish. Dickinson's explanation was that "it pleased the Lord to work wonderfully for our preservation."

The survivors made it known that they wanted to go north toward St. Augustine, but the casseekey insisted there were cannibals in that direction and, after a day and night of looting that left the men with only a pair of breeches or a coat each, the Indians marched them south. This was not, by any means, the last crisis the survivors would face before nineteen of them (Allen and four more slaves died north of what is now Daytona Beach) eventually reached Charles Town (today's Charleston), South Carolina, the nearest English town, on December 26. It did, however, set a pattern of Quaker passiveness that, judging by its results, was as good a tactic as any.

The party spent three days in the casseekey's village, a collection of huts made of poles bent to form domes and covered with palmetto thatch. The huts were atop a large shell mound on the south shore of Rio Jobe, undoubtedly the mound in DuBois Park. The mood of the Indians alternated between friendship and hostility, though they did seem to enjoy the Quakers' Bible readings, whether or not they could make any sense of the strange words they heard.

Finally disregarding the casseekey's warnings about cannibals, Dickinson and his party headed north on September 28, some in a leaky boat and others on shore. Two days later, they confronted a new group of Indians on the south shore of St. Lucie Inlet. Once again, they were stripped, called Nickaleers, and threatened with gruesome death. Once again, however, they were saved either by their passivity, Cresson's command of Spanish, or divine intervention. They were ferried across the inlet in canoes and put up for the night in the casseekey's house, which seems a bit like one of the "longhouses" occupied by a chief and his relatives in other areas. Dickinson described it as being "about forty foot long and twenty-five foot wide, covered with palmetto leaves both top and sides. There was a range of cabins, and a barbecue on one side and two ends."

During the night in this "strange and dismal" place, where "death seemed [to have] surrounded us," Dickinson was especially alarmed to hear "a strange noise which was not like unto a noise made by a man." The sound, he learned, was air escaping from a gourd as the gourd was dipped into a pot of a liquid made from the leaves of caseena, a holly-like shrub. This liquid, consumed only by the casseekey and his associates, apparently was the same purgative "black drink" used by Indians throughout the Southeast and to this day by Seminoles during their Green Corn Dance.

Late the next evening, after Indians visiting from the north had satisfied themselves that "most of us were Spanish"—though they clearly had their doubts about the light-haired members of the party—"we were on a sudden ordered to get up and hurried away." After a miserable night of walking north amid constant abuse from the guides, with only a two-hour stop during which no one could sleep because of the cold and insects, the group came upon the wreck of an English ship.

Shortly afterward, Dickinson's group was ferried across Indian River Inlet (roughly in the area of today's Pepper Park on the north beach of Fort Pierce) to meet the casseekey of Jece, who escorted them to his town on the east side of Indian River, south of today's Vero Beach. This was a much larger town than those Dickinson and his companions had visited, and here they stayed a month while the casseekey and Cresson went north to St. Augustine. During that time, they befriended the survivors of the other ship, which had run aground the same night as the *Reformation*.

The party's most frightening moment here came not from Indians, but from nature. A great storm, quite possibly a hurricane, nearly inundated the village. "We imagined that the sea was broke in upon the land, and that we should be drowned," Dickinson wrote. "The house was almost blown to pieces, and the Indians often a-tying and mending it." After two days, however, the water finally began to recede.

When Spanish soldiers arrived from St. Augustine, the Indians realized from the communication problems that their suspicions about the nationality of Dickinson's group were correct. The knowledge did them little good; the soldiers made it clear they would not tolerate mistreatment of either ship's company, and soon both parties were on their way north. Though Dickinson and his party met little more hostility from Indians, they were constantly short of food; they had brought little food with them, and the villages along the way didn't have much more to offer. Their weakened condition and the combination of hunger and cold proved more deadly than any aborigines had been. Shortly before the survivors reached St. Augustine, Allen and four slaves succumbed to exhaustion.

After recuperating for two weeks in St. Augustine and finding new boats, Dickinson and his party resumed their trek northward, reaching Charles Town the day after Christmas. Three months later, they sailed on to Philadelphia.

Dickinson lived twenty-six more years, during which he became a wealthy business and political leader in Philadelphia. He filled numerous public offices, including chief justice of the Pennsylvania colony and mayor of Philadelphia. Meanwhile, he shared his experiences. The first edition of his journal was published in Philadelphia in 1699. It became so popular that it was reprinted twenty-two times in English, Dutch, and German between 1700 and 1869. Keeping with the piety of its content, the full title of that first edition was "GODS PROTECTING PROVIDENCE MAN'S SUREST HELP AND DEFENCE. In the times of the greateft difficulty and moft Imminent danger. Evidenced in the Remarkable Deliverance of divers Perfons, From the devouring Waves of the Sea, amongft which they Suffered Shipwrack, And alfo from the more cruelly devouring jawes of the inhumane CANIBALS of FLORIDA."

Dickinson had more opportunity than had anyone else, either Spanish or English, to observe an otherwise little-known chapter of history. He seems to have been a good observer. And survivor.

Sources for this chapter include an oral presentation by amateur historian John R. Reis; *A Reexamination of the Fossil Human Skeletal Remains from Melbourne, Florida, With Further Data on the Vero Skull* by T. D. Stewart; "Little Salt Spring, Florida: A Unique Underwater Site" by C. J. Clausen et. al.; *Aboriginal Subsistence Technology on the Southeastern Coastal Plain during the Late Prehistoric Period* by Lewis H. Larson; *Fort Center: An Archaeological Site on the Lake Okeechobee Basin* by William H. Sears; "Father Juan Rogel to Father Jeronimo Ruiz del Portillo, April 25, 1568" by Father Juan Rogel; *Jonathan Dickinson's Journal* as edited by Evangeline Walker Andrews and Charles McLean Andrews; "The Barnhill Mound, Palm Beach County, Florida" by Ripley Bullen; *The Enterprise of Florida* by Eugene Lyon; *Memoir of Do. Escalante Fontaneda Respecting Florida* by Hernando d'Escalante Fontaneda; *A Survey of Indian River Archaeology, Florida* by Irving Rouse; "Report on the Indians of Southern Florida and Its Keys by Joseph Marina Monaco and Joseph Javier Alana Presented to Governor Juan Francisco de Guemes y Horcasitas, 1760" by Father Joseph Javier Alana; "Spanish-Indian Relations in Southeastern North America" by William C. Sturtevant; and *Prehistoric Peoples of South Florida* by William E. (Bill) McGoun.

The First Floridians

The Indian cultures Jonathan Dickinson had observed were on the verge of destruction, something he had no way of knowing. For thousands of years, these aborigines and their predecessors had maintained a stable way of life, only to disappear within a century of the Quakers' visit.

In 1913, canal-diggers in Vero Beach came across bones that appear to have been in the ground at least ten thousand years, making them almost certainly the remains of the area's first people. These people were big-game hunters who subsisted on large animals that today are extinct, such as the ground sloth, mammoth, and mastodon. Known as Paleo-Indians, they were either displaced by or evolved into the Archaic people, opportunistic hunters and gatherers who ate and made tools from what was available. This way of life would persist until it was disrupted by the Europeans.

It was not an easy life. There were probably fewer than ten thousand people in all of southeast Florida at the peak of the aboriginal cultures, just before European contact. What today is prime oceanfront real estate was for the Indians only a place to come occasionally to catch shark and other fish. They could not remain on the coast for long: storms, a lack of edible plants, and, most importantly, the absence of fresh water kept them inland.

Shark-fishing was worth the risks for these Indians, who lived in a land with no hard stone or metal. The teeth provided the hardest cutting tools; the vertebrae were used as ornaments; and the meat from one shark could sustain a band for days. Shellfish were also important for more than their meat. Various archaeological reports tell of pounders, scrapers, axes, adzes, picks, projectile points, hatchet heads, awls, ladles, spoons, and pendants made from shells. The mound in DuBois Park in Jupiter, half of which was carted away for road fill early in the 1900s, offers an idea of the quantity of shellfish gathered over the centuries.

Deer provided not only meat but bone for many uses, including hollow-tipped projectile points. Other resources include turtles, snakes, and various berries—notably sea grape—which were gathered and the roots possibly eaten. Food preservation came with the arrival of pottery, presumably introduced from the St. Johns River area to the north shortly before the time of Christ.

Our knowledge of aboriginal South Florida religion is limited, but we know a fairly elaborate ceremonialism apparently accompanied some funerals in the Lake Okeechobee area as early as the time of Christ, and we have some insights based on the writings of Spanish priests. Juan Rogel, a Jesuit who visited the Calusa people of southwest Florida during the 1560s, says the people believed in three souls, one of which remains in the body after death and can be consulted as an oracle. The "accustomed singing and dancing" Dickinson encountered at Jece probably was at least partly religious in nature.

By Spanish times, the bands in southeast Florida apparently had evolved into three groups. To the south, centered on Biscayne Bay and extending north through much of Palm Beach

County, was the Tequesta. Seventy-two graves dating from 700 A.D. to 1300 A.D. were found in the Barnhill Mound (near Federal Highway and Yamato Road in Boca Raton), the most famous Indian site in coastal Palm Beach County. In the 1950s, the mound was turned into a tourist attraction called Ancient America, but with the increase in development and the decline of U.S. 1 as a through highway, the attraction lasted only a decade, until 1966. A few miles to the north and east, about the same time as the Barnhill Mound burials, at least ninety people were interred in a mound near the ocean in what today is Highland Beach. But we do not know for sure that either of these sites was occupied by the Tequesta. The bodies could have belonged to a band that was later displaced by the Tequesta.

The DuBois Park mound probably marks the principal site of the second group, the Jaega, who presumably also lived in the St. Lucie Inlet village, while Jece undoubtedly was the main town of the Ais. Inland, a now-destroyed site within today's Belle Glade may have been a cere- monial center for smaller Indian sites, including one in the John W. Corbett Wildlife Management Area and another west of Boynton Beach.

Spanish contact in South Florida was sporadic. Juan Ponce de León cruised the eastern shore in 1513, putting in at Jupiter Inlet to gather firewood and naming the Loxahatchee River "La Cruz" (The Cross). His party was attacked by sixty Indians, typical of the hostility that greet- ed him at each landfall, which suggests that the real discoverers of Florida were slave traders who had preceded him. Attempts by the Spanish to establish missions at Charlotte Harbor and Biscayne Bay in the 1560s were short-lived. A garrison set up about ten miles from Jece in 1565 and relocated to Jupiter Inlet was abandoned within a year.

Juan d'Escalante Fontaneda, a Spaniard who was shipwrecked in Florida and lived with the Indians for seventeen years in the mid-sixteenth century, said, "The king of Ais and the king of Jaega . . . are rich . . . by the sea, from the many vessels that have been lost well-laden" with gold and silver. Fontaneda may never have seen either group and, in any case, overrated the affluence of both. The Indians' poverty and the fact that they were not amenable to a mission lifestyle due to their nomadism caused the Spanish to lose interest. But as long as the Indians did not mistreat shipwreck victims, the Spanish were willing to leave them alone.

Dickinson's account suggests that pre-Columbian lifestyles were intact in 1696, but we know from other sources that pressures from the north were increasing. From the moment Charleston, South Carolina, was founded as Charles Town in 1670, the English had encouraged the Indians under their influence to raid southward. This pressure was felt even in South Florida, which explains the Indians' hatred of Englishmen. But the Indians weren't all that crazy about Spaniards, either. Dickinson reported that a friar had been killed in the Cape Canaveral area about the time Dickinson had been in Jece and suggested the Indians' accommodation of the Spanish was due more to fear than amity. Still, the Spanish seemed to be less of a threat to the aboriginal way of life than were the English.

After Dickinson's time, the Ais and Jaega virtually vanished. There are no more accounts mentioning them, and, according to Irving Rouse of Yale University, there is no archaeological evidence of the Ais after 1700. It was suggested in 1737 that the Spanish establish a colony of two hundred in the Ais area to protect shipping lanes, but it is almost certain that those Indians were actually Yamasees from the north, not Ais.

By 1708, raiding parties are reported to have been as far south as the Florida Keys, and Tequesta Indians were being evacuated to Cuba. By 1743, when the Spanish made a final attempt to establish a mission on Biscayne Bay, the groups south of Lake Okeechobee had been reduced to one band of 180 that occupied the north bank of the Miami River seasonally, and three inland bands of no more than a hundred each. One of these was the Santaluces, for whom a high school on Hypoluxo Road is named. The Spanish also set up a short-lived mission in 1743 on Indian River, a little south of today's city of Fort Pierce. It soon was abandoned on orders from Havana and torn down so no one else could use it.

When the Spanish ceded Florida to the English in 1763, they took what they believed to be the last of the South Florida Indians—eighty families—to Cuba with them. Quite possibly, at least a few individuals remained, but they would be assimilated by the raiders from the north, who would come to be known as Seminoles. ❧

Chapter 2
William Jenkins Worth
Battling the Seminoles

William Jenkins Worth is commemorated in name in more places than are some presidents. In Palm Beach County, there is Lake Worth the lake, Lake Worth the city, and Worth Avenue in Palm Beach, none of which he ever saw. In Texas, there is the city of Fort Worth and a nearby lake named Worth. In New York City, there's Worth Street and Worth's grave surmounted by a monument, at Broadway and Fifth Avenue.

Who was Major General William Jenkins Worth? He was the sort of man around whom playwrights build tragedies, a man of great virtues and great shortcomings. He was handsome, trim, a fine horseman, and a fearless fighter. As John K. Mahon, history professor emeritus at the University of Florida, put it in his 1967 book about the Second Seminole War: "Could he have remained forever on the battlefield there probably would not have been a more famous officer in the service. Unfortunately, he had a petty streak mingled with overweening vanity, which cropped up when he was not in a fight."

He was praised justly by President John Tyler as the man who quickly ended the Second Seminole War after years of combat that was often marked by relatively desultory army efforts. In Mexico, he again fought bravely—his detractors would say recklessly—but began to dream of the presidency and got involved in intrigues that resulted in his arrest by General Winfield Scott, the same Scott who had championed Worth early in Worth's military career. He died of cholera at fifty-five, well away from the seat of power as the postwar commander of the Department of Texas.

Worth was born into moderate means in Hudson, New York, a river town south of Albany, on March 1, 1794. His father, Thomas, a Quaker seaman, held a colonial land grant. When the War of 1812 broke out, the teenager enlisted as a private, but it soon became evident that he had the talent to be much more. On March 19, 1813, he was commissioned as a first lieutenant, and soon he drew the attention of Scott, then a brigadier general, and became his aide-de-camp.

William Jenkins Worth.
(Library of Congress)

With Scott, Worth fought in July of 1814 in the battles of Chippewa and Lundy's Lane, two indecisive engagements that lifted American morale, coming as they did after a series of reverses. Both were wounded at Lundy's Lane, Worth so severely that it was feared he would die. Instead, he was confined to bed for a year and lamed for life. During the next twenty-seven years, Worth, who was allowed to remain in the army despite his disability, served in a variety of commands. For eight years (1820–1828), he was commandant of cadets at West Point, even though he had never attended the academy.

In the 1830s, a new war was brewing, this one against the Seminole Indians in the recently acquired territory of Florida. The roots of the Seminole nation go back to the founding of Charleston, South Carolina, when the English encouraged their Indian allies to raid southward. Such southward migrations of various Indian groups continued after the establishment of Georgia in 1732, during the British period in Florida (1763–1783), and into the second Spanish period. (Britain had captured Havana during the French and Indian War and exchanged it for Florida; the Spanish won Florida back by aiding the American colonies in their war for independence.)

By this time, the Indian refugees, mostly Creeks, had become known as Seminoles. Many sources say the name is a corruption of the Spanish word for "runaways," but Michael Gannon of the University of Florida says that the British took the name from the Creek word for "wild ones" or "separatists." In any case, the newcomers had, for the most part, free land after 1763. They got along well with the British, and the Spanish exercised virtually no control outside of St. Augustine during their second reign. As the nineteenth century dawned, it must have seemed to the Indians as if they had built a secure new life. It was not to be.

The new United States of America already was feeling the call of

Manifest Destiny. "Americans in the southern states coveted Spanish Florida," Mahon wrote. "They felt that Florida belonged to the United States as a foot belongs to a leg." There was another factor, too, one that cropped up in virtually every political issue of the antebellum South: slavery. Runaway slaves were finding sanctuary among the Seminoles, either in a more benign form of slavery or as free persons. "Whether slaves or free, the Negroes among the Seminoles constituted a threat to the institution of slavery," Mahon wrote. He spoke here of the second Spanish period, but his statement was no less true afterward. "How could human property be safe as long as red men remained in the peninsula?"

A series of incidents culminated in the First Seminole War of 1817–1818, during which forces under Andrew Jackson swept the northern portion of today's state with no regard for Spanish sovereignty, driving the Indians south and convincing Spain that it might as well cede Florida. The United States took over in 1821, with Jackson as first territorial governor, and the pressure on the Indians continued as white settlers moved into Florida. In 1832, some tribal leaders signed the Treaty of Payne's Landing, pledging that the Seminoles would exchange their Florida lands for an equal area in the west. Other Seminoles denounced the treaty. Tensions grew. On December 28, 1835, a force of 108 officers and men commanded by Major Francis L. Dade was ambushed north of Tampa Bay; only three survived. War was on.

What followed was what usually happens when a conventional army from outside takes on guerrilla bands who know their country well. The Seminoles did not have the numbers to challenge army troops in pitched battles, so, after suffering heavy losses in the Battle of Okeechobee on Christmas in 1837, they never fought that way again. And things didn't go very well for the army. As a matter of fact, the largest single capture of Indians, 531 of them, was made under a flag of truce in February of 1838 at Fort Jupiter, located on the Loxahatchee River probably west of the FEC Railway bridge. And small bands were still holding out three years later, when Worth took charge of the campaign.

As Captain John T. Sprague, author of the most complete account of the war (and later Worth's son-in-law) wrote, "The progress of the Florida war . . . was attended with large expenditures of money, and serious embarrassments. The climate, ignorance of the swamps and hammocks, and the treachery and activity of the enemy, baffled the skill of the most zealous and intelligent officers." That probably is true. But it also appears to be true that not all of the officers in the Florida campaign were zealous or intelligent. It was, in a modern phrase, a dirty little war in a far-off place with no visible rewards and the constant threat of sudden death in an ambush. Some military efforts were halfhearted. And the troops did not take the field at all during summer's heat.

By this time, Worth had become a brevet colonel, which means he had a colonel's responsibilities but not a colonel's pay. When he took command in Florida in May of 1841, his soldiers soon knew a new era was at hand. He ordered an immediate summer campaign with the terse words: "Find the enemy; capture or exterminate." When Major Thomas Childs lost patience trying to use the captured Chief Coacoochee to persuade other Indians to surrender and shipped Coacoochee to New Orleans en route to Oklahoma, Worth became enraged. He ordered Coacoochee returned to Tampa Bay, the military headquarters, and through the chief effected the surrender of four hundred Indians within five months. His methods of persuasion were blunt. On shipboard in Tampa Bay, he told Coacoochee that if the five Indians he was to send out did not bring in the rest of his band, Coacoochee and the others in custody "should be hung in the yards of this vessel."

Meanwhile, military operations were pressed aggressively. The Indians were pursued throughout the state. In December, the army mounted the first major operation deep into the Everglades. For two months, columns crossed and recrossed the swamps. Few Indians were encountered, but the psychological effect was great. As C. R. Gates of the Eighth Regiment put it, the soldiers "drove the Indians out, broke them up, taught them we could go where they could." Gates went on to reflect about the toll taken on the soldiers: "Men and officers worn down; two months in water; plunder on our backs; hard times; trust they soon to end." They soon did.

On April 19, 1842, with Worth personally commanding a company of dragoons, the last major Seminole resistance ended with the rout of Halleck-Tustenuggee's band at Peliklakaha Hammock, near Lake Apopka. On August 14, Worth declared hostilities concluded. Of course, decreeing that a war has ended is one thing and persuading a nonliterate people divided into small bands with no means of inter-

WARFARE ON THE LOXAHATCHEE

During most of the Second Seminole War, the southern part of the state was a backwater. For three months in 1837–1838, however, the area east of Lake Okeechobee was critical. During that time, the largest single battle and the largest single capture of the war brought to a close large-scale Indian resistance, though the war would drag on for four more years, until Worth declared it ended in 1842.

In late 1837, two years into what—until Vietnam—would be the nation's longest war, brevet Major General Thomas Sidney Jesup determined the United States could pin down the Indians in South Florida by constructing a chain of forts across the state. The easternmost link was forged in November when Lieutenant Colonel Benjamin Kendrick Pierce built a stockade on the west bank of Indian River, south of Indian River Inlet. As was customary, the fort was named for him, as is the present-day city a mile and a half north of it.

Pierce, today aptly described as "the obscure brother of an obscure president [younger brother Franklin, elected in 1852]," was at the time somewhat better known than his sibling. He had been promoted from major three months earlier for "distinguished service" in a battle at Fort Drane (between today's Gainesville and Ocala), during which a force of five hundred Indians was routed. But Fort Pierce's place in Second Seminole War history is marked not by what happened there but rather by operations launched there and by the names of those stationed there. Noteworthy were Captain Joseph E. Johnston and Lieutenant William T. Sherman, later famous commanders for the South and the North, respectively, in the Civil War.

To the west, however, a bigger battle was brewing. Troops under the command of president-to-be Colonel Zachary Taylor were pushing the Indians into a difficult decision, one that would be crucial to the war's progress. The winter planting season was approaching, and the Seminoles had nowhere to plant. They had been driven from their fields in North Florida and backed into unsatisfactory cropland east of Lake Okeechobee, land that still is good only for pasture. Taylor's brigade was approaching from the west. The Indians, four hundred strong, decided they must stand and fight. They set up an ambush in a hammock about seven miles southeast of today's Okeechobee City, near U.S. 98-441 and the creek that bears Taylor's name.

Their surprise was foiled on Christmas morning when Taylor's column captured a Seminole who told of the plan. Taylor lined up his troops across the swamp in which the Indians were hidden and, shortly after noon, attacked. The battle was furious. In addition to bows and arrows, the Seminoles had firearms and ammunition obtained from whites both before and during the war. The first wave—Missouri volunteers commanded by Colonel Richard Gentry—was driven back with a withering fire during which Gentry was mortally wounded. Then the first line was caught in a crossfire as regular troops to the rear opened fire on the Indians. The regulars were hit hard as they, too, tried to advance. They were persistent, however, and after an hour, the Indians, who disliked this type of fighting, began to give way.

Statistics suggest that the army got the worst of it—26 killed and 112 wounded, as compared to 11 Indians killed and 14 wounded—but the statistics miss the point. Never again would the Indians attempt such a stand against the soldiers, since they could not afford to lose so many. The army could always call in new recruits, but there were no more than one thousand Seminole men left from which to draw replacements.

That's not to say the Indians wouldn't fight if they felt it was necessary, as they did several times in the Everglades. The worst of these engagements was on January 15, 1838, in swampy land near the Loxahatchee River headwaters. Approaching an encampment in the swamp, army troops were met with heavy fire that drove them back. Five were killed, fifteen wounded. In response, Jesup led a column south from Fort Pierce. Approaching the Loxahatchee from the west on January 24, Jesup heard that a large force of Indians was waiting in a hammock ahead, ready to fight. Anxious to prove himself in battle, the general ordered an attack. The Indians quickly gave way across the river. Seven soldiers were killed and thirty-one wounded in what would be known as the Battle of the Loxahatchee. Seminole losses never were determined. Both battles probably took place in the Riverbend Park area, west of the turnpike on Indiantown Road.

Jesup's men then built Fort Jupiter, a stockade that almost certainly was on the Loxahatchee west of today's railroad bridge. The new fort succeeded Fort Pierce as headquarters for Jesup's Army of the South. From there, Jesup communicated with Fort Dallas (today's Miami) over a military trail on the approximate site of the present-day highway of the same name. According to retired judge and local historian James R. Knott, one of the army's guides in the Jupiter area was an Indian named Chachi, who lived in the vicinity of today's Palm Beach Mall.

As was true of commanders before and after him, Jesup decided that further pursuit of the Indians into the Everglades was pointless. After a parley with several Indian leaders, he agreed to recommend that Washington call the whole thing off. The Indians, tired of the fighting and optimistic that Jesup's suggestion would be heeded, encamped near the fort. Ceremonies of peace were held, and soldiers even joined the Indians in a rousing spree of dancing and drinking in the Indian camp. The reply came on Saint Patrick's Day. In terse language, Secretary of War Joel R. Poinsett said "no."

Truce or no truce, Jesup decided he had gone through too much trouble to let the Seminoles melt back into the wilderness. Troops surrounded the encampment and seized more than five hundred Indians, 151 of whom were warriors. It was the largest single capture of the war, and never again until modern tribal fairs would that many Indians be gathered in one spot in South Florida. ❖

communication to stop fighting is another. In the Panhandle, where raiders had killed two settlers on August 11, "the orders of Col. Worth . . . occasioned [the people] to doubt, for the first time, the forecast and ability of the officer, who, in so short a space of time, had rid the country of its most numerous and formidable foes," Sprague said. Nevertheless, the war, for all practical purposes, was over. Halleck-Tustenuggee, the last effective war leader, had surrendered. In any case, Worth was an ambitious man who had no intention of squandering his career chasing small bands of Indians through the swamps.

Worth did not, however, get out of Florida that easily. Except for a trip to Washington to be made a brevet brigadier general and to hear praise from Tyler for "gallant and distinguished service," Worth remained in Florida as military commander until war broke out again, this time in the Southwest as Manifest Destiny ran head-on into Mexican sovereignty. Worth's ego got him into trouble even before the fighting had started. He lost his temper and resigned his commission in October of 1845 when passed over as second in command to Scott in favor of a colonel. He withdrew his resignation, however, when war became imminent and once again distinguished himself in the field. He became a brevet major general after his crucial role in the United States victory at Monterey. Congress by resolution presented him with a sword.

Then the fighting wound down, and Worth got into trouble again. Angered by Scott's criticism of Worth's governorship at Puebla, a city east of Mexico City, Worth challenged an order by Scott restricting private accounts of military operations. Scott had Worth arrested. The incident blew over, but Worth's rise up the military ladder was over. He was made military commander in Texas, a post he held until he died in San Antonio on May 7, 1849.

Meanwhile, the first non-Indian settlers along Florida's Treasure Coast were having their own problems.

This chapter is adapted from *History of the Second Seminole War* by John K. Mahon; *Appleton's Cyclopedia of American Biography* as edited by J. G. Wilson and John Fisher; *The Origin, Progress, and Conclusion of the Florida War* by John T. Sprague; *History of the Second Seminole War* by John K. Mahon; and files of the St. Lucie Historical Museum and the St. Lucie County Library.

Chapter 3
Mills Olcott Burnham
Occupation of the Frontier

Mills Olcott Burnham came to the territory of Florida to regain his health. His recovery was so successful that Burnham became a man admired for his strength. He was first a frontier sheriff, later a legislator, then a wilderness homesteader. In this last role, he became a leader in the first non-Indian community along the lower Indian River, a settlement that was born of the spoils of war and survived economic reverses and an Indian attack to lay the foundation for today's St. Lucie County.

Burnham was the sort of industrious person who could make a go of it away from civilization. While at the Indian River settlement, he reportedly was the first to raise pineapple commercially in Florida and the first to successfully ship turtles north. He was the sort of settler Congress had in mind when it passed the Armed Occupation Act of 1842 in August of that year, the same month General William Jenkins Worth declared the Second Seminole War at an end.

The act was proposed by Senator Thomas Hart Benton of Missouri in 1840 as a means of securing the new southern frontier. It provided for 160-acre grants to homesteaders who would erect a dwelling, cultivate a minimum of five acres, and remain on the land for seven years. The homestead could not be within two miles of a fort, and the owner was responsible for holding it against the Indians. Land offices were set up in Newnansville (near today's Gainesville) and St. Augustine as settlers began moving into the Alachua prairie, the St. Johns River valley, and the Indian River area. One of the first attracted to the Indian River was a Jacksonville gunsmith named Burnham.

Burnham was born on September 8, 1817, in Thetford, Vermont. He lived as a youth in Troy, New York, where he learned his trade at the Watervliet Government Arsenal, and in 1835 he married Mary McEwan. Two years later, believing he had a lung disease, he came to Garey's Ferry (near Jacksonville) to see if the climate would help his condition. Whether it did is conjecture, but his health improved, and in 1839, he sent for his wife and son.

Not long after the Armed Occupation Act passed, the St. Augustine land office began validating claims—283 of them—including those for the St. Johns River valley. Twenty-one claims were reported on or near Lake Worth (there is no further knowledge of them), but most of those on the coast were in the Fort Pierce area. Some forty-six claims were validated for that portion of the Indian River from Sebastian River south nearly to the Loxahatchee River. And, by the end of 1842, the first settlers were on their way south. Among them were Ossian B. Hart, who became governor during Reconstruction, and Burnham.

Some of the settlers at first took shelter in the abandoned Fort Pierce, built in 1838 during the Second Seminole War, but on December 12, 1843, the buildings there burned "and with them the supplies of every description laid in by the settlers sufficient for the consumption of several years," according to an account from that time. The pioneers were hardy, though, and by spring, their homes and farms had come far enough along for them to organize a community, which was called Susanna.

Most of the settlers apparently lived in the three-mile stretch along the west shore of Indian River from Midway Road (State Road 712) south to Ankona Road. Besides planting fields and planning their community, the settlers of Susanna tied their frontier to the outside world. They dug a canal connecting Indian River with Mosquito Lagoon in the Titusville area to facilitate inland commerce, and they built a customs house at Indian River Inlet (then, as in Jonathan Dickinson's time, north of today's Fort Pierce Inlet). In 1844, they opened the St. Lucie Inlet.

Federal laws that had been passed at the end of the Second Seminole War barred Seminoles from the area, but the Indians stayed on anyway. Fortunately for the settlers, the Indians were friendly, despite their recent hostility. They were particularly fond of Burnham because of his marksmanship and his ability to make and repair firearms. The Indians were on such good terms with him that they used his homestead as a trading post when they visited the settlement. Burnham liked the Indians, but his wife was terrified of them, so he asked the Indians not to come around whenever he had to leave the settlement, and they complied.

So now, the settlers had safety and transportation to go with their moderate climate. There was just one problem: They couldn't make

Mills Olcott Burnham.
(Frank Childers)

a living. Consider the story told by Caleb Lyndon Brayton, a settler whose letters to his wife provide much firsthand information about Susanna. In July of 1844, he listed a score of food crops and expressed hope "to make several hundred dollars" from fish and roe. But by October of 1848, he wrote, "my evil star still predominates," after telling of setbacks in the fish and turtle businesses. The citrus trees grew too slowly to pay back the homesteaders' investments for several years, and there was no alternative cash crop to carry them. Despite the shipping routes, produce could not make it to northern markets before spoiling. And neither cotton nor tobacco could be grown profitably.

In 1847, there were only twenty-four men left in the settlement, including Burnham. He supplemented what he could make farming Ankona Bluff—and, with pineapples, he was more successful than most—by entering the green turtle business. He would catch the turtles, which were plentiful in the river, and take them to Charleston in his schooner, *Josephine*. Others such as Brayton had tried this, generally with little luck because the turtles would be dead or dying by the time they had reached Charleston. Burnham solved this problem by devising wooden pillows to support the necks of the animals and by having his crewmen wash out the eyes of the turtles each morning with saltwater. His cargo would arrive in good shape, earning top dollar. He was away on one of those trips that July day in 1849 when the Susanna era ended in violence.

According to one version of the incident, some Indians had become unhappy with a trader named James Barker and took revenge because they believed he had been cheating them. Another version, which seems more likely in light of subsequent events, is that a group of troublemaking renegade Indians visited the settlement and attacked at random. At any rate, four Indians came upon Barker and his brother-in-law, customs collector William F. Russell, working in their fields near Sebastian. "All four took deliberate aim and fired on them," according to a letter written by Brayton two weeks later. "One ball passed through the left arm of Colonel Russell fracturing the smaller bone and slightly grazing his abdomen. Then they threw down their guns and pursued Mr. Barker who ran for the house. They succeeded in overtaking him a short distance from the house where they stabbed him, causing his immediate death."

Settlers just south needed no other encouragement to leave. "Captain Gattis took Colonel Russell in his boat and pushed off," Brayton wrote. "Another gentleman and myself launched another boat which lay on shore and were just pushing off when eight Indians came up within twenty-five paces and took deliberate aim over a fence and fired on us. One ball passed through the sleeve of a negro man in the boat with us. They reloaded and again fired at us, but none of the shots took effect. Before they could reload again we were out of reach."

Brayton made a quick—very quick—visit to his house. "I got my guns and ammunition but did not stop to get my papers or clothes. I then repaired to the boat and went all over the settlement, wading ashore at every house. . . After alarming all the neighbors and getting them into small boats, we launched a small schooner boat of about three tons in which we put all the women and children and what things they could gather up in the hurry and hustle of the moment and anchored her off in the stream."

By sea and by land, the settlers fled north. All reached St. Augustine safely, though not reassured. Mrs. Burnham and her children "had so little time to prepare for the journey that they left without their hats . . . and all suffered much from the hot August sun," Robert Ranson wrote in an account of Burnham's life. "What course I shall take I don't know being without a cent of money and only the clothes I stand [in], which are now beginning to give way," Brayton wrote. "Government I presume will immediately establish a garrison at Indian River. In that event I should wish to return and look after my effects."

Brayton was right. Within six months, Fort Capron was established (at the site of today's St. Lucie Village) with a garrison of five hundred. The force, Brayton wrote, "renders it perfectly secure near the garrison, though I do not consider it safe to go to my place to live which is some nine miles distant." Meanwhile, one of the four Indians in the Sebastian attack, Hoithlemathla Hajo, was killed by Seminoles attempting to capture him and turn him over to the army.

Another of the raiders, Kotsa Eleo Hajo, was deported to Oklahoma. The fates of the other two, Panukee and Seh-tai-gee, are not known.

The name Susanna went into temporary eclipse with the Indian raid but, contrary to many previous reports, the settlement survived. "It looks like a New England village here, all is bustle and activity," Brayton wrote on January 25, 1850. "The Sound is white with sail. Buildings are going up daily. Vessels are in the stocks. Three stores are open. Teams are moving in every direction. Roads are being constructed. A splendid road is nearly completed from here to Tampa Bay and a military post established every 10 miles the whole length of it. . ."

Susanna had been the seat of St. Lucia County since its creation in 1844, and it remained the seat under the name Fort Pierce until 1855, when the county was renamed Brevard and the seat's name changed to Susannah. St. Lucia County was far larger than today's St. Lucie County, extending from Hillsboro Inlet north to Cape Canaveral on the coast, inland to Lake Okeechobee, and as far northwest as Lakeland. The 1850 census showed twenty-two heads of families in St. Lucia County, suggesting that most of the Susanna settlers had returned. Brayton mentions that the Russell family had come back.

Burnham, though, was not among them. He did not come back south until 1853, and that was only as far south as the Canaveral lighthouse, of which he became the keeper. With the exception of the Civil War years, when Confederates darkened all Florida lights, he kept the Canaveral light burning until he died in April of 1886. He also had a farm nearby where he raised oranges, pineapples, bananas, sugarcane, and corn, succeeding in agriculture in an area where many before him had failed. The orange grove was his pride, and it is where he was buried.

The reborn Susanna prevailed, another lighthouse was built to the south, and keepers on the Loxahatchee River established the first permanent settlement in what today is Palm Beach County.

This chapter incorporates information from *Pictorial History of St. Lucie County, 1565-1910* by Kyle S. Van Landingham; "The Indian River Settlement: 1842-1849" by Joseph D. Cushman Jr.; "The Indian Scare of 1849" by James W. Covington; "The Story of 'Susanna'—First White Settlement in What Is Now St. Lucie County" by N. W. Jorgensen; *East Coast Florida Memories, 1837 to 1886* by Robert Ranson; "Destruction of Fort Pierce" (anonymous article); and "A New Englander on the Indian River Frontier: Caleb Lyndon Brayton and the View from Brayton's Bluff" as edited by Edward Caleb Coker and Daniel L. Schaefer.

Chapter 4

James Arango Armour
Keeping the Light at Jupiter

In Jupiter in the nineteenth century, the Jupiter lighthouse, its iron cage 105 feet above a small hill, was the only man-made object visible to a sailor until he pulled his boat up to the foot of the hill. Then, the coquina-rock house and oil-storage shed came into view. Otherwise, there was nothing. Across the channel to the south was the large shell mound that had been home to a Jaega Indian village when Jonathan Dickinson and his party had shipwrecked in 1696. But there were no Indians there anymore; the Jaega had died out a century before. Aside from scattered bands of Seminoles—left over from a number of wars and near-wars—who mostly roamed inland in search of food, there may have been no humans within thirty miles.

If Almeda Catherine Carlile had been looking for a quiet honeymoon in December of 1867, she found it. If she had been looking for a sometimes adventurous life on the frontier, she found that also. For forty-one years, as first river boats and then rail lines opened up southeast Florida to the outside world, her husband, Captain James Arango Armour, would tend the light at Jupiter to warn vessels of the reef offshore. If the warning were to no avail, he would help the survivors to shore. And his wife, despite some disquieting moments, would learn to cope.

The lighthouse sat on part of the Fort Jupiter reservation, established during the Second Seminole War of 1835–1842. With the peace that followed the war, though, this log palisade on the bank of the Loxahatchee River (probably in the Riverbend Park area) soon reverted to its natural state.

James Arango Armour.
(The Palm Beach Post)

Armour, born on September 5, 1825, in New Amsterdam, New York, was one of many settlers who drifted to Indian River once the hysteria set off by the 1849 Indian attack at Susanna had worn off. He already knew a lot about the sea from service on clipper ships, but you didn't have to know much to know the sea was treacherous off southeast Florida. Southbound ships had to stay close to shore to avoid the northbound Gulf Stream. In a storm, they could easily get too close and go aground. Northbound ships, such as Dickinson's *Reformation*, were not much better off, because the Gulf Stream that carried them is often within a mile of shore in Palm Beach County. As a result, the sea was studded with wrecks ranging from the Spanish treasure ships that lured salvors to the sea bottom, to the Union Army supply ships that sank off Fort Pierce's South Beach, to an assortment of late nineteenth-century wrecks that spewed ashore everything from sewing machines to coconuts.

No spot on the coast was more dangerous than Jupiter, with its off-shore reef. Thus, in 1853, the federal government authorized the construction of a lighthouse there. It would be seven more years, however, before the light would be lit, due to the logistics of supply and the intervention of yet another Seminole war. First came the design, executed by a then-obscure army officer named George Meade, later known for being the general who won the Battle of Gettysburg in the Civil War. Construction began in 1855, the same year that callous surveyors destroyed the garden of Billy Bowlegs in southwest Florida and set off the Third Seminole War. Though this conflict had no effect on the lower East Coast more notable than the renewed use of Fort Capron (at the site of today's St. Lucie Village), the fear of an Indian attack nevertheless was enough to halt construction. For many years, until the lighthouse was painted red, a change in brick color showed where work had been discontinued during hostilities. By 1858, the so-called Billy Bowlegs War had ended with the deportation to Oklahoma of most of the remaining Indians, and work on the lighthouse had resumed.

One of the hardest parts of the project was transporting the materials. Jupiter Inlet was narrower and shallower—as well as farther south—than today's artificial channel, which was dug in 1921. It also frequently silted up to the point that it could not be used and had to remain closed until inland water pressure built up sufficiently to blast the sand loose. Thus, materials had to be unloaded at Indian

River Inlet, near Fort Pierce, and brought down Indian River on barges. The last ten miles were through Jupiter Narrows, a shallow, winding creek that, in places, was only twenty inches deep.

In all, five hundred tons of material had been moved before the lighthouse was completed in 1859 at a cost of $60,859.98, almost twice the original appropriation of $35,000. On June 12, 1860, the oil lamp was lit by Thomas Twiner. Through a series of lenses, the light was intensified to produce a beam visible eighteen to twenty-seven miles away. Twiner kept the light until January 1, 1861. Then J. F. Papy took over, until the Civil War came to Jupiter.

The Civil War arrived in a bloodless manner. At the outbreak, Confederate sympathizers urged Papy to extinguish the light, so it would not help Union ships spot blockade runners. Papy professed sympathy to the South but said he could not bring himself to shut down the proud new light that had been put in his charge. Then, on an August night, he was confronted by a group of men who removed enough parts from the light to make it unserviceable, though undamaged. The same group went on to Cape Florida and shut down that light, the last one still operating in Confederate territory.

Though the light was dark throughout the war, signals reportedly came from the tower to let blockade runners know the coast was clear. The ships would sail in—the inlet remained navigable during those years—and load or unload to the north on Indian River. Some runners undoubtedly were captured by the Union patrol boat *Sagamore*, which had on board a volunteer pilot who was very familiar with these intricate waterways, James Arango Armour. Armour, one of the few Union sympathizers in the area, was busy during the war. Shortly after the lighthouse had been shut down, he found the missing parts in a palmetto hammock and took them to Key West, where he remained for a while as keeper of prize ships. His service on the *Sagamore* earned him several letters of commendation.

With the coming of peace, a federal agent was sent to Jupiter to reopen the lighthouse. Armour brought the missing parts from Key West and signed on as an assistant keeper under William B. Davis. The next year, he married Almeda Carlile in LeGrange, near Titusville, and, the year after that, became keeper when Davis gave up his post. There were to be no more wars, Indian or otherwise, for nearly a century, but Jupiter still was a wilderness. And the Indians would be frightening to anyone not used to them, though they certainly were not menacing.

The Armours' youngest child, Bertha, recalls the day her mother opened the door to find a large Indian carrying a knife in his teeth. It was of no use to scream: Armour and his assistants had gone to the beach. Anyway, she was too frightened to scream. Then the Indian removed the knife from his mouth and handed it to her, handle-first, signifying friendship. He soon helped her to understand that he simply wanted permission to camp on lighthouse property for a few days. A greatly relieved Mrs. Armour granted his request. That would not be the only surprise. Many times over the years, she would look up from what she was doing to find an Indian standing silently beside her. It was something to which she never quite became accustomed.

A pair of tremors, the only earthquakes ever recorded in south Florida, threatened the Armour home and the lighthouse on January 12, 1879, but both rode out the scare without damage. In 1883, a second house was built; before then, the Armours had had to share the single structure with both assistant keepers and their families. In 1886, a life-saving station was established to the south (in the area of today's Carlin Park), and Charles Carlin took charge of it. (In the 1870s, Houses of Refuge for shipwrecked sailors were built on Hutchinson Island near today's Stuart and on the beach north of today's Atlantic Avenue in Delray Beach.)

Carlin's skills helped make the decade from 1886 to 1896 the safest for sea travel in the Jupiter area in centuries, according to Jupiter historian Bessie Wilson DuBois. He and his crews would brave crashing seas to carry vital supplies to distressed ships or to ferry survivors to shore. On other occasions, they would put rollers under a beached craft and pull it landward out of the reach of the waves.

By now, a new age had begun. The first of several so-called Barefoot Mailman routes along the beach, including one from Jupiter south to Miami, was active as early as 1870. And there were enough people in the area by 1884 to demand that the Jupiter post office be reestablished, with Armour as postmaster (the post office at Fort Jupiter had been discontinued before the Civil War). Even more settlers had homesteaded to the south along Lake Worth. To supply them with the goods they needed, steamboats were plying Indian River from Titusville to Jupiter by 1890, though they became obsolete only four years later when Henry Flagler extended his Florida East Coast Railway south to Palm Beach. In 1895, much of the Fort Jupiter

Jupiter Lighthouse in the 1870s.
(The Palm Beach Post)

reservation was opened to homesteading, and that same year, dredging began on what would become the Intracoastal Waterway.

Jupiter was still a small community. But there were a number of homes—a map shows twenty homesteads in the area by 1911—a school, and two bridges over the Loxahatchee River, one for the railroad and the other for the first Dixie Highway. The highway bridge was west rather than east of the rails, as it is today. The lighthouse station's first radio transmitter, a sign of things to come, was set up in 1905.

The lighthouse remains in use, though today radio beacons are more important than lights for ocean navigation. And ships still wash ashore on occasion. The most famous wreck of recent years was the freighter *Amaryllis*, driven onto Singer Island during Hurricane Betsy on September 9, 1965. All attempts to refloat it failed, and eventually it had to be cut apart by a wrecking crew. A Venezuelan freighter named *Mercedes* was stuck for 105 days on the beach just south of the Kennedy estate in Palm Beach from 1984 to 1985.

When Armour retired from his lighthouse duties in 1908, after coming into a substantial inheritance two years earlier, he turned over the facility to his son-in-law, Joe Wells, and moved to a large, two-story home he had built west of the railroad. There he died, on July 8, 1910. For forty-eight years, until Wells left in 1914, manning the light at Jupiter was a family affair.

Information in this chapter comes from "Saga of Mollie and the Mercedes To Make Silver Screen" by Sallie James; "Jupiter Lighthouse," "Two South Florida Lighthouse Keepers," and *The History of the Loxahatchee River* by Bessie Wilson DuBois; and an interview with Bessie Wilson DuBois.

Chapter 5
The Spencer Family
Pioneers on the Lake

The wind had veered to the northwest and had freshened considerably. . . . They started to beat their way back up the lake . . . with the wind constantly growing stronger and more northerly.

Then a black cloud began to show at the southwest. As it grew higher and higher, in spite of the gale that was raging, they decided to go to the west shore and camp. But over went their boat to windward. . . .

"Where are you, Father?" were Mattie's first words as she came up some distance from the boat. But so dark was it that she could not tell in what direction [the boat] was from her.

"Here, holding to the stern of the boat. Where are you?"

With a few strokes, she too had hold of the boat when it began to sink, thus proving that it would not support both. When the boat came up . . . out drifted the little box in which was the precious petition. Mattie caught it, poured the water out, set it on its bottom and let it go.

After great effort they got the mast and sail out of the boat and cut the anchor loose. Three times they righted it and bailed, only to have it capsized anew by the force of the waves. The last time they lost their bailer, to which they had clung before.

They then gave up trying to right the boat and took turns resting and swimming for three long hours before they reached the west shore.

Thus were the perils of establishing a post office on Lake Worth in 1880. Mattie Spencer, author of the chronicle, had accompanied her father, Valorus Orlando Spencer, on a sailboat trip around the lake to collect signatures on a petition for postal service. More correctly, it was for renewed postal service. There had been a mail route from the Fort Pierce area to Miami during the Civil War, but it had been

Valorus Orlando Spencer.
(Beth Spencer)

discontinued. The Spencers' petition asked that the route be reopened as far south as Lake Worth—the lake, not the city—and that a post office be established there.

That day, January 16, 1880, had dawned sunny, so the Spencers left their home on what is now North Lake Trail in Palm Beach and headed down the east shore of Lake Worth to "the foot of the lake," in the Hypoluxo area. Everyone they met signed gladly. Until then, mail had been sent south from the Fort Pierce area whenever a boat was going in that direction, and that might be only once every six weeks.

Hypoluxo settlers urged the Spencers to stay overnight because of the storm, but they elected to head back home, so the rest of the family wouldn't worry. When father and daughter finally reached shore after their spill, they were about a mile and a half south of Benjamin Lanehart's homestead, the only one on the west shore. (That would put them between Southern Boulevard and Belvedere Road in today's terms.) Lanehart put them up for the night, and in the morning, he and V. O. walked back to the spot he and Mattie had come ashore. The boat also had come to rest there, as had the box containing the petition.

After V. O. collected the signatures of the rest of the Lake Worth settlers, he sent the petition off to Washington. On May 30, the route was ordered reopened, and the post office was established, with V. O. as postmaster. The mail was brought by sailboat down Indian River to Jupiter. A carrier—the first of whom was Ed Capron—took it down the beach to the north end of Lake Worth, then by rowboat to the post office in V. O.'s home.

Pioneer living was nothing new to the Spencers. Their forebears had been on one frontier after another for 250 years. Jonathan Spencer and his three brothers, all younger sons of the Earl of Spencer, came to Massachusetts Bay between 1630 and 1632, only a decade after the Pilgrims. Later generations lived in upstate New

York and then in north-central Pennsylvania, when those areas were wilderness. Valorus Orlando Spencer was born in 1824 in Tioga County, Pennsylvania, near the border of New York, and moved south to Lake Worth after hearing favorable things about the area from his son, Melville Evans Spencer.

The first of the family to come to Florida, M. E., at twenty-five, had headed to Titusville, at the north end of Indian River. Undeterred by reports that no non-Indians lived between there and the Jupiter lighthouse, 130 miles south—in fact, there were some settlers in the Fort Pierce area—he headed south in 1875, walking the beach all the way. When he arrived, he was in luck; lighthouse keeper James Arango Armour needed an assistant. The Jupiter lighthouse then was near the north end of a county that extended from the Florida Keys all the way to the St. Lucie River, an area so large the county sometimes was called the "State of Dade."

Melville Evans Spencer.
(Beth Spencer)

Spencer stayed about a year, demonstrating his competence with a camera by taking photos that provide the best visual record of Jupiter Inlet in the late nineteenth century. Nevertheless, the frontier still called him south—not too far this time, however. At the lighthouse, Spencer kept hearing of a paradise several miles to the south, a clear lake surrounded by lush tropical growth and a beautiful, sandy, ocean beach. In 1876, he quit his lighthouse job and homesteaded a large tract in what is now the north end of Palm Beach.

He was not the first on the lake. There may have been a score of settlers as early as 1842 under the Armed Occupation Act. It's certain a man named Lang moved south from Indian River to escape Confederate service in the Civil War and built a house in the area of the present Palm Beach Inlet, where he lived with his wife until 1868. One story has it that he dug the first inlet into what had been a freshwater lake, then moved away because the saltwater had killed the lake's fish. Though they didn't stay long, six Confederate fugitives headed by Secretary of War John Breckinridge camped the morning of June 4, 1865, on the beach just to the north of today's town of Palm Beach. The six, who would ultimately make their way to Cuba, ate a breakfast of turtle eggs before pushing on southward.

An old sailor named Charlie Moore moved into the Lang house in 1872. The first homestead of the area was granted in 1873 to Hiram F. Hammon, who lived several miles south. And Hannibal Dillingham Pierce, another assistant keeper at the Jupiter lighthouse, soon followed, picking out a tract on Hypoluxo Island. Six more families, including the Laneharts, had also moved there before 1876, when Spencer joined the growing community.

As had the others, Spencer built his home on the lake. The ocean was fine for recreation, but the pioneers wanted their homes sheltered. Besides, they were farmers, and you couldn't grow crops on the beach. The island was much different then than it is today. The parts that were high and dry were covered mostly in palmetto scrub; the Australian pine had not been introduced and there were only a dozen coconut palms. Extending from today's Breakers Country Club south to the Worth Avenue area was a large sawgrass swamp. But life there was good. In fact, Spencer's letters home were so glowing that, on January 16, 1878, the elder Spencer arrived by schooner with his wife, Jane, and daughters Florence and Mattie. He homesteaded a tract just south of his son's land.

The next month, there was another arrival: a profusion of coconuts that would give the town-to-be its name. The Spanish bark *Providencia* had run aground (just south of what now is the Bath and Tennis Club) with a cargo that included twenty thousand of the giant seeds from which the coconut palm grows. Such a windfall was not all that unusual. Aside from farming, the most lucrative occupation was salvaging wreckage. Many of the early homes were underpinned with timber from ships and outfitted with all sorts of items salvaged from shipwrecks. After all, the nearest general store was in Titusville, and lumber had to be brought from Jacksonville— no easy task since for the final twenty miles of the journey, there was no navigable inside passage south of Jupiter, and boats had to finish the trip on the ocean.

It's tempting to try to romanticize the wilderness and to picture those early Lake Worth settlers constantly risking life and limb in a savage land. But that's not the way it was. The soil and climate around Lake Worth were excellent, allowing the settlers to grow almost all of their food—some even tried coffee. And game and fish were plentiful. The few Seminole bands who had remained in South Florida had no desire for further combat. In later years, M. E. Spencer said, "We always found [them] to be honest, kind and friendly people." And, though it is true there were bears and panthers, they were few in number and anything but a serious threat. The face-to-face encounter M. E. Spencer had with a black bear was more humorous than anything else, according to an account written by his grandson, Melville Louis Spencer:

In walking the beach early one morning after a nor'easter, looking for anything that may have been washed ashore, he came upon a large buoy. . . . He walked around [it] and as he did so he met a huge black bear. Neither was aware of the other's presence until they met face-to-face a few feet apart. Grandad looked up—frightened and surprised—no doubt jumped a foot or two in the air—shouted and waved his arms wildly. The bear, as startled as Grandad, reared upon his hind legs, lost his balance and toppled over backward. Grandad, with the element of surprise on his side, continued shouting and stomping the ground. The bear regained his footing and started running back down the beach in the direction he had come.

Mattie Spencer Heyser.
(Beth Spencer)

As the 1880s progressed, clusters of homes began to form around the lake. Allen E. Heyser, later a county judge and the husband of Mattie Spencer, bought a little more than eighty acres near the north end of the lake in 1882. He built a home and, in 1888, the Oak Lawn House (later Oak Lawn Hotel). One year later, Oak Lawn opened a post office, where Mattie served as postmistress. Supposedly at the inspiration of a journalist who had called the area the "Riviera of America," the post office name was changed to Riviera in 1893.

South County Road in Palm Beach as it looked in the nineteenth century.
(The Palm Beach Post)

The first of the Lyman family settled on the west shore opposite Hypoluxo Island in 1887. Two years later in his general store, M. B. Lyman opened the first post office in the community he would come to call Lantana, after the ornamental shrub. In 1890, Samuel and Fannie James received a federal patent for land north of Lantana and a post office, under the name of Jewell, in what would later be the city of Lake Worth. The area's first schoolhouse—since preserved and moved to Phipps Ocean Park—opened in 1886 on the lake in the northern part of today's Palm Beach.

The Spencers remained prominent in the area through four generations. Besides being the first postmaster in the area, V. O. operated the first United States Department of Agriculture experimental station in South Florida. In 1894, M. E. ran the first steamboat on Lake Worth, the twelve-passenger *Night Hawk*. Among other things, M. E. towed lumber rafts from Juno to Palm Beach for Henry M. Flagler's Royal

Poinciana Hotel. Later, he sold his Palm Beach holdings piece by piece as the island became a premier resort.

M. E. Spencer's daughter-in-law, Wilma Bell Spencer, was society editor of the *Palm Beach Daily News* for twenty-seven years. Her second book, a collection of reminiscences, was published posthumously in 1975. And M. E.'s grandson, Melville Louis Spencer, starting with little money after World War II—the crash of 1929 had hit the Spencer family hard—built Spencer Boat Company into an area leader in its field. He ran the firm until his death in 1973. Looking east from the boatyard, he could see a row of palatial homes sitting on what nearly a century before had been two pioneer homesteads.

This chapter is based primarily on unpublished accounts written by various members of the Spencer family and on an interview with Bertha Spencer, widow of Melville Louis Spencer.

Chapter 6

Andrew Walton Garnett
Mailman on the Beach

In 1885, three young Kentuckians joined the wave of settlers flocking to the shores of Lake Worth. Their goal was to make their fortunes as citrus growers at the south end of the lake. Andrew Walton Garnett lived there for fifty-five years, farming extensive tracts on and near Lake Worth and on Lake Osborne, and becoming, at various times, the county treasurer and a member of the Dade County School Board. But today, few persons outside the old-time families know who he was. James L. Porter didn't do as well as Garnett—though he was moderately successful—and is even less well known. James Edward Hamilton died within two years, but he has been remembered as the legendary "Barefoot Mailman."

It's doubtful that these three men had expected to become legends when they arrived that August day on the west shore opposite Hypoluxo Island and bought adjoining six-acre tracts for two hundred dollars each. Since none of the men was married, they built and initially shared a single wooden home with a palmetto-thatch roof. Their arrival helped make the new farming community large enough to earn its own post office, which Garnett saw as a chance to make some money until his first crop came in. He became postmaster, setting up his office on a small, homemade table in the northeast corner of the house, but it didn't work out. He soon realized that the job required more time than it was worth and was keeping him away from his fields too much. At first, he turned the work over to his assistant, Charles William Pierce, then resigned in September of 1887 in favor of Pierce's father, Hannibal Dillingham Pierce.

With the new post office open, the beach-walking mail route from Jupiter to Miami, which had been in operation since the 1870s, was split. In 1887, Hamilton won the first Hypoluxo-Miami contract for six hundred dollars a year.

A lot of legend has grown up around the Barefoot Mailman since publication in 1940 of Theodore Pratt's book of that name. It's not Pratt's fault; he never pretended his novel was factual. The "wild, roadless southeast coast" to which Pratt referred in his introduction was roadless but not that wild. For a young man in good physical condition, the trip was nothing more than an easy, three-day walk each way, with overnight stops at the Houses of Refuge for shipwrecked sailors at Orange Grove (Delray Beach) and New River (Fort Lauderdale). If there were any bloodthirsty salvors, as in Pratt's novel, none of the mailmen ever saw them.

The mailman had to walk because, although he could carry or find enough freshwater for himself, there was no way to provide enough for a horse. He walked along the edge of the water, where the sand was packed hard, and did so barefoot with his trousers rolled up because the saltwater would rot his shoes. But he never called himself a "Barefoot Mailman." That name originated with Pratt's book. The mailman carried his belongings, and a locked canvas mail pouch, on his back in a black oilcloth knapsack. Sometimes, he even had "passengers," people who paid five dollars each for the escort and the use of government boats where the water was too deep to cross. Only in three places was that the case, at Hillsboro and New Rivers and on Biscayne Bay.

Hamilton made most of the trips himself. Whenever he couldn't, either Garnett or Charles Pierce filled in. The tall Hamilton—just under six feet—left Hypoluxo for the last time on the morning of October 10, 1887, a Monday. He stayed overnight with Stephen N. Andrews, keeper of the Orange Grove House of Refuge, and continued south on Tuesday. Hamilton should have returned to Orange Grove on Friday. When he hadn't come by Saturday morning, Andrews headed north to notify the town that the mailman was missing and to deliver his House of Refuge report to Palm Beach. At Hypoluxo, Andrews gave the report to Garnett to pass on, then headed back south to search for Hamilton.

At Hillsboro Inlet, Andrews found Hamilton's knapsack hanging on a bush, with the mail pouch intact inside. Hamilton's clothes were scattered along the beach. The boat was tethered to the opposite shore. No trace of the mailman's body ever was found. Hamilton apparently had arrived at the inlet to find the boat on the wrong side of the passage and tried to swim across to retrieve it. The river was especially high due to heavy rains inland, so he might have drowned, or possibly he was attacked by a shark or an alligator. The cause of his death is a matter of speculation.

*One of six murals by artist Steven Dohanos depicting the story of the Barefoot Mailman.
The murals are displayed at the main branch of the West Palm Beach Post Office.*
(The Palm Beach Post)

A southbound traveler who had shown up at New River House of Refuge about the time Hamilton had disappeared was charged with tampering with government property. He was accused of moving the boat even though it had a sign warning not to do so. But the charges were dropped for lack of evidence. Garnett and Pierce finished Hamilton's contract, and Garnett later won the contract on his own. But, for him, all of this was interim; his love was the land.

Hypoluxo doesn't look today as it did when Garnett came south; neither does his hometown of Cadiz, Kentucky. Cadiz now has the recreational advantages of Lake Barkley, created by the Tennessee Valley Authority, and the payroll of a large military installation nearby. In the years after the Civil War, it was much poorer. Garnett's parents died as he was approaching maturity, and he was just past twenty when, with Hamilton and Porter, he went to seek his fortune. The three went first to nearby Paducah, then south to Florida's Gulf Coast. They arrived in Bartow in January of 1885 and soon purchased property south of Fort Myers. When they heard about the fertile, frost-free farmland on Lake Worth, they changed their minds and headed east. They liked the look of the sand and muck soils— mostly sand in the Lantana area—and bought.

"It's difficult in this age of machinery to imagine the immensity of the task of clearing land, planting and, after harvesting, getting the produce to a market," said Margaret Harris, Garnett's daughter. "Hired help and mules were unavailable or in very scarce supply, and mosquitoes [were] everywhere." Getting the produce to market continued to be a problem throughout the next decade. At first, the goods had to be shipped to Jacksonville by ocean, with perhaps part of the trip on Indian River, a hazardous journey in any craft small enough to enter the shallow inlets of those days. If the cargo did make the trip successfully, it frequently had rotted long before then. And, because almost everything was shipped on consignment, the grower got nothing.

It was not until 1893 that an all-inland route was established, and this involved shifting the cargo three times. Lake boats would take the produce to Juno, at the north end of the lake, where it would be loaded onto the narrow-gauge Celestial Railway that connected Juno with Jupiter and stopped at now-forgotten stations known as Mars and Venus. At Jupiter, the goods were loaded aboard large river steamers for the trip up Indian River to Titusville, the railhead of Henry M. Flagler's Jacksonville, St. Augustine, and Indian River Railroad.

But this arrangement would be short-lived, for Flagler was on the move. Renamed the Florida East Coast (FEC) Railway, the railroad reached Palm Beach in 1894 and Miami in 1896, putting the Celestial Railway—built in 1888—out of business in less than a decade. Garnett immediately saw the advantage of the FEC. He even donated some land to Flagler and talked his neighbors into doing the same, which some of them held against him in later years. Besides being able to ship their produce north without transfers, the farmers now could get their goods to Miami in a single day. The Bay Biscayne Stage Line,

Andrew Walton Garnett.
(Margaret Garnett Harris)

which had supplanted the beach mailmen in 1892, involved a two-day trip from Hypoluxo, with an overnight stop at New River.

By the time the FEC came through, Garnett had become one of the largest landowners in the area. He had started to build up his holdings in 1886, when he and Porter each homesteaded 160-acre tracts west of their lake property (west of what now is U.S. 1), Garnett's on the north side of Hypoluxo Road and Porter's on the south. Garnett got away with keeping the property, even though his home was along the lake, by building a humble second home there and staying in it each year for precisely the number of nights required under homestead law.

He used this land, drier than the land along the lake, for pineapples. Then, in 1894, he purchased for four hundred dollars a sixty-acre tract on the east shore of Lake Osborne—then known as "the freshwater lake"—in the area that today is between Lantana and Hypoluxo roads. Here, he put in citrus. He also built a packing house along Lake Worth. A later one stood until the 1970s on the east side of U.S. 1 at Hypoluxo Road.

For Garnett, 1896 meant a lot more than seeing the rails extended to Miami. That summer, he went back to Kentucky to visit relatives and met Lillie Mae Morehead, a schoolteacher who was staying with Garnett's sister. On October 6, they were married. To cap the year off, Garnett was chosen to serve a two-year term as Dade County treasurer. That and a four-year term immediately following on the Dade County School Board were his only ventures into public office. He was a community leader in other ways, however, especially in religion. A devout Methodist, Garnett was one of four Hypoluxo pioneers who took turns using their homes for Sunday school.

In addition to his cash crops, he raised much of the family's food, including five kinds of bananas, avocados, guavas, watermelons, pineapples, and mangoes. Pineapples had been an important cash crop in the early years. But, after Flagler extended his railroad to Key West in 1912 and gave preferential rates to Cuban shippers to get their business, the crop no longer was economical commercially.

Garnett ran his various agricultural operations until the mid-1920s, when he turned them over to his oldest son, Irl. He remained active until he broke his hip in a fall in 1936. He was unable to attend the dedication ceremony on October 10, 1937—fifty years from the day Hamilton last left Hypoluxo—of the marker at Hillsboro Inlet commemorating Hamilton's service. Porter couldn't attend, either. The night before, he had suffered a stroke that soon led to his death.

The tale of the three Kentuckians ended less than three years later, on April 6, 1940, when Garnett died. By that time, there were eighty thousand people in Palm Beach County, most of them living near a lake that had only a handful of settlers half a century earlier.

The primary source for this chapter is an interview with Margaret Garnett Harris. Additional information comes from *Pioneer Life in Southeast Florida* by Charles William Pierce.

Chapter 7
The Chillingworths
Murder on the High Seas

For most people, the name Chillingworth brings to mind the death of Circuit Judge Curtis Eugene Chillingworth, who with his wife Marjorie was brutally murdered in 1955 at the orders of a former West Palm Beach municipal judge. Few people realize that at twenty-six, he became the youngest circuit judge in Florida and that he was credited with making major contributions to the evolution of the law during his thirty-four years on the bench. Not many people know his father, Charles Curtis Chillingworth, was the first municipal attorney for both West Palm Beach and Lantana and developed the Martin County community of Palm City. Or that his grandfather, Richard Jolley Chillingworth, was sheriff of Dade County from 1896 to 1901, the first mayor of the city of West Palm Beach, a West Palm Beach councilman, and a justice of the peace.

Richard, born in England on November 30, 1833, was only a year old when his parents brought him to the state of New York. The fam-

Richard Jolley Chillingworth.
(The Palm Beach Post)

ily settled in the Oswego area, but Richard later took his dreams to the California gold fields. On April 25, 1865, he married Eunice Ann Bettinger. A little more than three years later, on May 12, 1868, they had their only child, a boy they named Charles Curtis. In 1891, C. C., who had graduated from Cornell University in 1890 and had studied law in Atlanta, migrated to the north end of Indian River. He was admitted to the Florida Bar on February 9, 1892, and was hired by a Titusville law firm to open an office in Juno, the seat of Dade County.

At that time, Dade County comprised today's Miami-Dade, Broward, and Palm Beach Counties, as well as most of Martin County and some of Okeechobee County. It had all of nine hundred residents. Miami, its largest single settlement, was the seat for most of the county's history, except for a ten-year span after the Lake Worth area swayed the vote in an 1889 referendum and the court-house moved to Juno (near today's intersection of PGA Boulevard and U.S. 1). The two-story, white frame structure, forty feet by sixty feet, dominated the Juno landscape of low sand hills spotted with palmetto and some pine. In one of its three ground-floor rooms, C. C. set up his law practice.

In 1894, Henry Flagler completed his Royal Poinciana Hotel in Palm Beach and extended his Florida East Coast Railway south to a point opposite the hotel on the west side of Lake Worth. To provide housing for his employees, Flagler bought the O. S. Porter property along the west side of the lake for thirty thousand dollars and laid out a town with forty-eight blocks. The settlement soon became the preeminent community on the lake, and on November 5, seventy-eight residents met and voted—77 to 1—to form a town called West Palm Beach.

Charles Curtis Chillingworth.
(The Palm Beach Post)

C. C. Chillingworth, who became the new town's attorney, married for the second time the following year (his first wife, Annie Seabrook Whaley, had died after giving birth to a healthy son, Walter Seabrook, in 1893), and the new Mrs. Chillingworth, Jennie Dietz of Syracuse, New York, gave birth on October 24, 1896, to the first of three children, a son they named Curtis Eugene.

In 1903, West Palm Beach was reincorporated as a city, and C. C.'s father Richard—who had followed his son south and had been on the council for two years—became mayor, while his son branched out into development.

The younger Chillingworth formed the Palm Beach Land Company and in the autumn of 1910, purchased twelve thousand acres southwest of Stuart, on the west bank of St. Lucie River's south fork. Palm City would be his only venture into real estate. Otherwise, he stayed with the law until retiring in the early 1930s.

By this time, the law firm had a new name: C. C. and C. E. Chillingworth. Curtis Eugene was a bright young attorney on the fast track to success. He had graduated from Palm Beach High School in 1913, in the first class to take all its courses on the Sapodilla Avenue campus that now houses the Dreyfoos School of the Arts. November of 1920 was a busy month for C. E.: on the second, he was elected county judge, and three days later, he wed Marjorie Crouse McKinley. He spent two and a half years on the county bench until appointed circuit judge, the state's youngest, on June 13, 1923.

Over the next three decades, he built a reputation as "one of the great trial judges in Florida history," according to former United States District Judge Charles Fulton, who practiced before C. E. as a trial attorney. The judge was not a gregarious man. His life was devoted to the law and to his family. In his book *The Murder Trial of Judge Peel*, Jim Bishop says, "Judge Chillingworth was a meticulous, humorless man. . . . Some say he had exactly seven friends."

Curtis Eugene Chillingworth.
(The Palm Beach Post)

Marjorie Chillingworth.
(The Palm Beach Post)

The Chillingworths lived comfortably but not ostentatiously. Besides their home on Dyer Road in West Palm Beach, they had a beach house inside the curve where State Road A1A meets the ocean north of Boynton Inlet in Manalapan. In winter, they rented the house to vacationers; in summer, they used it quite a bit, especially on weekends. On June 14, 1955, a Tuesday, they dined with a few friends at their home before going to the beach house for the night. When two carpenters who had been hired to repair a window frame arrived at the beach house the next morning, they found no one at home. Then they noticed red spots on the wooden stairway that led down to the beach and footprints in the sand. They called the judge's secretary, who called the sheriff's office. Within an hour, Sheriff John F. Kirk and all the officers he could round up were on the scene.

Apparently, the Chillingworths had spent the night at the beach house, because the two beds in one of the bedrooms were rumpled. And, by afternoon, it had been established that the spots on the stairs were blood of Mrs. Chillingworth's type. But except for the fact that there was also a broken outside light, that was all police knew. And that would remain all they knew for five long years.

Not that there weren't suspicions. Neither State Attorney Phil O'Connell Sr. nor West Palm Beach Police Lieutenant William Barnes, later chief, had much respect for Joseph Peel, an eager young lawyer who split his time between private practice and a part-time municipal court post as judge. In 1953, Judge Chillingworth had publicly reprimanded Peel for his unethical handling of a divorce case and had warned him that if it happened again, he would recommend disbarment. It happened again. A similar complaint was pending at the time of the judge's disappearance.

Still, that wasn't a good enough motive for murder. As Joseph White, who was the county's only other circuit judge in 1955, pointed out, "(Peel) should have known . . . another judge would have been appointed to hear the charges." That's exactly what happened. In September of 1955, Circuit Judge Lamar Warren of Fort Lauderdale—Palm Beach and Broward Counties shared the Fifteenth Circuit at the time—suspended Peel from the practice of law for ninety days. Peel then resigned his judgeship, and in 1958, with new charges pending, he resigned from the bar.

But suspicions don't put anyone in jail. Evidence does. And police didn't have evidence, even though some suspected Peel might be

Police examine abduction scene, Manalapan, in June of 1955.
(Sam R. Quincey)

irrational enough to order the killings and that a friend of his, another glad-handing type by the name of Floyd "Lucky" Holzapfel, might be mean enough to carry them out. Investigators hadn't found out yet that Peel had supplemented his income by protecting gambling interests. After signing a search warrant as municipal judge, he would call the suspects and warn them of the raid for a fee, an extreme example of the kind of abuse that led Florida to abolish municipal courts in the 1970s.

The first major break in the Chillingworth case came in 1958 when, while investigating the murder of a moonshiner named Lew Gene Harvey, Henry Lovern of the Florida Sheriffs' Bureau got a tip that Peel might be tied to the Chillingworth killings. The tipster was a bail bondsman named Jim Yenzer, suspected with Peel and Holzapfel the year before of plotting to kill Harold Gray, Peel's law partner, for insurance money. But nothing had been proven.

Information came slowly through months of dogged undercover work, but it did turn up. By 1959, Lovern had become reasonably sure Holzapfel and George David "Bobby" Lincoln of Riviera Beach had murdered both Harvey and the Chillingworths, the latter under Peel's orders. But it would be another year before there would be enough evidence to move against Peel. First, Holzapfel was lured into a seventy-hour drinking spree in a Melbourne motel, during which he admitted his role. Agents in the next room recorded the conversation. Then Lincoln, serving a federal term for moonshining, was granted immunity and brought back to Palm Beach County secretly to reenact the crime. On October 4, 1960, Peel was arrested and charged with murder.

On March 7, 1961, Peel went on trial in Fort Pierce after arguing successfully there had been too much publicity in Palm Beach County. The trial lasted seventeen days. With Lincoln as the key witness, the state told what happened the night of June 14, 1955. Lincoln and Holzapfel took a boat from Riviera Beach to the shore in front of the Chillingworth house, knocked on the door, and abducted first the judge and then his wife when they answered. The light was shattered so the area would be dark. The Chillingworths were tied up and led toward the beach. When Mrs. Chillingworth screamed, Holzapfel hit her over the head with his pistol, causing the cut from which the spots of blood had come. Two miles offshore, the weighted bodies of the Chillingworths were thrown overboard. Just before his wife was thrown into the sea, C. E. worked his gag loose and said, "Honey, remember, I love you." "I love you, too," she replied.

Peel was convicted of the murder of C. E. and later pleaded no contest to the murder of Mrs. Chillingworth. After serving eighteen years of his life sentence, he was transferred to federal prison to serve a term for an unrelated mail-fraud conviction. On June 25, 1982, terminally ill with lung cancer, Peel was paroled into the custody of the woman he had married nine days earlier. Just nine days after that, on July 2, he died in her Jacksonville home.

Holzapfel pleaded guilty and was sentenced to die, but his sentence was commuted to life in prison several years later. He remains in prison. Lincoln was set free after serving his moonshining term. After spending some time out of state, he returned to Palm Beach County under the name David Kareem.

Sources for this chapter include a family history written by Charles Curtis Chillingworth and *The Murder Trial of Judge Peel* by Jim Bishop.

SIX-SHOOTER POLITICS

Charles Curtis Chillingworth's introduction to South Florida politics would have been enough to discourage most people. His first Dade County political convention, in 1892 in the two-story frame courthouse that once marked the Juno landscape, nearly ended in a shoot-out. The flavor of the times is captured best by Chillingworth's own words, as recorded in a 1932 article he wrote concerning the history of the Masonic order in today's Palm Beach County:

There were two very strong rival factions in the Democratic party in Dade County. One was dominated by certain active Democrats residing at Juno and on Lake Worth. The other was dominated by Democrats living at Jupiter and north of Jupiter. A bitter feud existed between these factions. Each was determined to control the party in Dade County and to ignore the other.

In those days there were no primaries. Each settlement had a caucus or neighborhood meeting at which delegates were chosen to a county convention to be held in the county courthouse. As the time for holding this convention in the fall of 1892 approached, dire threats were made by each faction against the other. Each faction was determined to organize the convention with its own men. Fraud in the selection of delegates was charged and the factional feeling ran high. It was predicted a few days before the convention that there would be bloodshed in the courthouse if both factions tried to organize the convention.

At the appointed hour quite a number of adherents of each faction assembled in the courtroom and each undertook at the same time to elect a chairman of the convention. Bitter taunts were exchanged and violent language used. I believe it is a fact that practically every man in the convention had either one or two guns upon his person. Our beloved clerk of the court, Albert F. Quimby, who was a man of most peaceable disposition, sat with his six-shooter over his knees covered with a handkerchief. Others were equally ready for action.

As the quarrel between the two factions grew hotter and hotter, it did look as though the first shot might be fired at any moment. I believe I was about the only man in the convention unarmed and I stood near the rear stairway ready to dive down to the ground floor as soon as the shooting began.

At this critical juncture one noble old patriarch, Jacob T. Earnest, of Lantana, arose on the south side of the room. He had perfectly white hair and a long, flowing white beard, and he always reminded me of a picture of Socrates. In a low, quiet, easy, smooth voice he began to entreat the men to cease their bitter language and to listen. . . . He had apparently talked only a few seconds before his dramatic appearance commanded respect. He then appealed to the 35 or 40 men present . . . to be calm and listen to reason. . . .

He said that he abhorred the thought of violence in word or deed. He told them that if it was impossible for the entire assemblage to organize into one convention that the only sensible thing to do was to let each faction organize its own convention, put up its own candidates and then fight it out at the polls.

The remarkable appearance of this good man brought the others to their senses. At once the Jupiter faction organized its own convention in the northeast corner of the room and the Lake Worth faction organized its convention on the south side of the room. Each put up its own candidates, and through this remarkable personality and the soothing words of this good old man, bloodshed was averted.

But the election which followed did not do away with the bitterness of the two factions because one faction lost all of its candidates and the other side won everything. ❖

Chapter 8

Henry Morrison Flagler
Father of Modern Florida

"A truth about American money men that many earnest people fail to grasp . . . is that the chase and the kill are as much fun as the price, which you then proceed to give away." Alistair Cooke was speaking of Andrew Carnegie when he said this, but the statement applies to Henry Morrison Flagler as well. Flagler spent half of his adult life seeking wealth. He succeeded far beyond the dreams of most people as John D. Rockefeller's chief aide during the formation of Standard Oil, then spent the rest of his years blazing trails with ventures from which he never recouped his investment. Though Sidney Walter Martin, Flagler's biographer, was being hyperbolic when he wrote, "Ponce de León's visit to Florida in 1513 was hardly more significant than Flagler's first trip there late in the 19th century," Flagler can be considered the man who opened up the east coast of Florida.

When Flagler came south in the winter of 1877–1878, he went no farther than Jacksonville because of poor transportation. When he

Horse-drawn car at Flagler's Royal Poinciana Hotel, circa 1924.
(The Palm Beach Post)

died thirty-five years later, his Florida East Coast Railway stretched from Jacksonville to Key West, with spurs to Lake Okeechobee. But Flagler built more than just railroads; he built cities. His crowning achievement sits on the east shore of Lake Worth, where he turned a group of farms into one of the world's most famous resorts. On the island, he built the Royal Poinciana Hotel, one of the world's largest wooden buildings, then the first Breakers Hotel. He linked them to the mainland with a rail bridge in the area of today's Flagler Memorial Bridge. On the mainland, he laid out for the hotel help a town that became West Palm Beach. Finally, he placed along the lake a magnificent structure—as much a museum and a place of enter-tainment as a home—for his third and last wife.

This is not to belittle Flagler's other accomplishments as a builder. He made St. Augustine into a modern city and laid out on the shores of Biscayne Bay a town called Miami. In between, his Model Land Company sold off tracts that would become a number of other com-munities, including Boynton (now Boynton Beach) and Linton (now Delray Beach). Thousands of acres elsewhere were sold for agricul-ture.

Through it all, he was a man more concerned and more generous with construction than with maintenance. As for materials, "Permanence appeals to him more strongly than to any other man I ever met," Edwin Lafevre said in an *Everybody's Magazine* article in 1910. "He had often told me that he does not wish to keep spending money for maintenance . . . but to build for all time." Lafevre also gave insight into the Flagler style: "He never gives positive orders. He expresses his views or wishes; but he also asks their views and invites suggestions. If theirs are better, he promptly says: 'That's better than mine. We ought to do that!' That's as near a positive order as he ever gives, and yet he is a man of decision and indomitable will."

Flagler showed that indomitable will at a young age. He was not yet fifteen when he left his family in upstate New York in 1844 to join his older half brother, Daniel M. Harkness, in business near Cleveland. The trip took weeks by boat and on foot, and he had only four pennies and a French nickel left when he arrived. Starting at five dollars per month, plus room and board, he worked his way up quickly and at twenty-two, had saved enough to become a partner in the Harkness grain and distillery business. On November 9, 1853, Flagler married Mary Harkness, a first cousin of his half brother.

Henry Morrison Flagler.
(Henry Morrison Flagler Museum)

The next decade was up and down; he made a lot of money in the Harkness business, but lost all of that and more when a salt-mining venture in Michigan collapsed at the end of the Civil War. So Flagler went to work for a Cleveland grain merchant and shortly thereafter reconnected with an acquaintance from his days with the Harkness firm, another grain merchant named John Davison Rockefeller.

By this time, though, Rockefeller had given up grain for a new field: oil. He and Samuel Andrews, who had the technical expertise, had organized a refining company in 1864 to cash in on this "black gold," which was used as it came from the ground for medicine or refined for heating or light. By 1867, business was so good that Rockefeller needed capital to expand. He got a hundred thousand dollars from Mrs. Flagler's wealthy cousin, Stephen V. Harkness, on the condition that Flagler have control of the investment. Thus, Flagler entered the oil business.

Standard Oil's business practices—notably that it froze out rivals and used financial clout to force railroads to give it rebates on all oil shipments, even those of competitors—would make Rockefeller a figure of revulsion in later years. Though Flagler unquestionably participated in the company's policies, he is not associated today with what was bad about Standard Oil, probably because he had withdrawn from an active role in the company before the worst facts came to light.

Mrs. Flagler's health already was deteriorating by the time Standard Oil operations were moved to New York City in 1877. She died on May 18, 1881. Afterward, Flagler was less concerned with making money, although his extensive Standard Oil holdings continued to increase rapidly in value. In 1883, Flagler embarked on a period that would include his most lasting achievements and his greatest personal sorrow.

On June 5, 1883, Flagler married Ida Alice Shourds and took her to St. Augustine for their honeymoon. (The second Mrs. Flagler, who had been one of Mary Flagler's attendants during her final illness, was a lavish spender and a would-be social lioness.) The honeymoon trip convinced Flagler, who had never liked cold weather, of the great potential of Florida tourism, and the development of Florida became his goal. By 1890, he had built a standard-gauge railroad as far south as the Daytona Beach area. In St. Augustine, he had built two hotels and had remodeled a third. The crowning jewel was the Ponce de León Hotel (today Flagler College), opened in 1889. The sprawling, four-story building had cost $2.5 million and had been designed in the style of Old Spain, with verandahs and landscaped gardens. It had 450 rooms and suites and a then-novel feature: electric lighting.

For his family, he constructed Kirkside, a winter home near the hotels, though the Flaglers didn't move in until March of 1893. Flagler apparently had thought his work would end there. He had received state approval in 1892 to lay rails as far as Biscayne Bay, but he had had no plans to go beyond Rockledge (near today's Cocoa) on Indian River. Two visits to the future Palm Beach—the second in 1893—changed his mind.

At that time, Palm Beach was still a collection of farms. Flagler realized that with a railroad and a hotel it could be much more. So he planned the Royal Poinciana Hotel and decreed a race between it and the rails. The railroad had been completed to Rockledge on February 27, 1893. On June 26, rails went to Eau Gallie (today part of Melbourne), and on January 29, 1894, trains were rolling into Fort Pierce. On March 22, the rails continued to a point across Lake Worth from the hotel.

But the hotel (on the site of today's Palm Beach Towers) had won. It was completed on February 11, after only nine months of work. The building materials, including five million board feet of lumber, had been shipped down Indian River by boat to Jupiter, on the narrow-gauge Celestial Railroad to Juno, then by boat again to the hotel site. The six-story Royal Poinciana had 540 rooms at first; later construction would add half as many more. In 1896, Flagler completed a rail and foot bridge across the lake and built a second hotel, the Palm Beach Inn, on the ocean. The inn was enlarged in 1900 and renamed The Breakers.

But Flagler was not to stop there. He was aware that the freeze of 1894–1895 had not damaged vegetation south of New River. Swayed

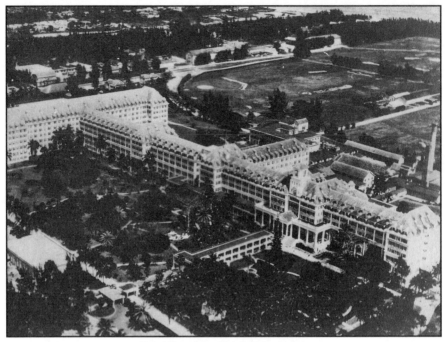

Royal Poinciana Hotel, Palm Beach.
(The Palm Beach Post)

by Julia Tuttle, a Biscayne Bay pioneer who agreed to give him land for rail yards, a depot, and a hotel, Flagler promised on June 12, 1895, to extend the rails to Miami. The extension was completed in just ten months.

During this time of public achievement, Flagler's private life was anything but happy. As early as 1894, Alice Flagler became delusional. She believed she was the fiancée of the czar of Russia and expressed homicidal tendencies toward her husband. Eight months in a sanitarium in 1895–1896 arrested her condition but not for long. A year later, she was institutionalized permanently and on August 4, 1899, was declared incompetent.

Flagler knew he wanted to divorce Alice and marry Mary Lily Kenan, a thirty-two-year-old North Carolina belle whom the Flaglers had known for some time. There was one big hurdle, though: neither New York nor Florida allowed divorce on grounds of insanity. The Florida Legislature changed that in 1901 by passing a bill to permit divorce on the basis of insanity of four years' standing, provided that the rights and material well-being of the insane spouse were safeguarded.

The bill was not enacted without controversy. It was widely assumed that Flagler had "bought" the law, and his gift soon afterward of ten thousand dollars for a gymnasium at Florida Agricultural College in Lake City (soon to be moved to Gainesville and renamed the University of Florida) was thought to be the price. In any case, Flagler lost no time. He filed for divorce on June 3, and seven days after the decree was granted on August 14, he announced his engagement to Miss Kenan. Ten days later, they were married at her family home in Kenansville, North Carolina.

For his new wife, Flagler needed a new home. Like her predecessor, the third Mrs. Flagler craved wealth and excitement. Whitehall, the home he built her for $2.5 million, would satisfy her desires. Marble steps lead past six towering pillars to brass gates that open into a 110-by-40-foot marble entrance hall. The rest of the building, with rooms ranging in style from Francois I to American Colonial, is equally magnificent. Besides family rooms, the second floor originally included sixteen guest bedrooms, each designed in a different period.

When Whitehall was completed in 1902, Flagler was seventy-two and white-haired. He still had one major project ahead of him, however: the Railroad that Went to Sea. Ignoring the advice of friends who said a Key West extension of his Florida East Coast Railway never would pay for itself—they were right—Flagler announced his plans on July 31, 1905, and work began. The target date was January 1, 1908, but it was four years later to the day, after delays due to both topography and storms, that the work was completed.

On January 22, Flagler was aboard the first train to officially make the trip. He was feted for days in a festive Key West, tied to the mainland for the first time. But Flagler was past eighty-two and growing feeble. His eyesight and hearing were bad, and he was nearly an invalid. A year later, on January 15, 1913, he fell down the last three steps of Whitehall's marble staircase and broke his right hip. After four bedridden months, marked by occasional rallies, he died on May 20.

The only one of Flagler's major Palm Beach buildings still standing is Whitehall, which has been open as a museum since 1960. The Royal Poinciana Hotel was damaged severely in the 1928 hurricane and torn down in 1936. The first Breakers burned down, as did the second. The present building was built in 1925. The overseas railway is gone, victim of the Labor Day hurricane of 1935, though the over-seas highway was built in many places upon rail-bridge pilings.

What remains are two things. The first is the Flagler name, com-memorated in streets and bridges, cities and counties. The other is Palm Beach. Where else would a famed architect such as Addison Mizner and his backer be expelled from the club they built? Where else would a family such as the Kennedys, that produced a president and three senators, remain on the fringe of acceptance? In the words of Theodore Pratt, "That was Palm Beach." Still is, in many ways.

This chapter was compiled from the files of the Henry Morrison Flagler Museum and from *Florida's Flagler* by Sidney Walter Martin.

Chapter 9
Edward Riley Bradley
Thoroughbreds and Roulette Wheels

A small green park on the north side of Royal Poinciana Way at the east end of Flagler Memorial Bridge held for forty-seven years one of the world's most exclusive gambling casinos. Evening clothes were required after seven o'clock. Married employees were not allowed to have their wives living with them, lest pillow talk lead to public knowledge of what went on within the shingled walls. And no one who was under twenty-five or who lived in Florida could enter.

Presiding over the Beach Club—through a hurricane in the 1920s and a U.S. Senate investigation during the 1930s, and despite state laws banning casinos—was a tall, distinguished Kentucky colonel who would give away thousands rather than allow a breach of decorum. Edward Riley Bradley told the Senate investigators, "I am a gambler and will bet on anything."

He was, however, much more. His Idle Hour Farm in Kentucky was home to horses who won almost a thousand races, including

Beach Club casino.
(Mort Kaye)

four Kentucky Derbies, and at least $2.5 million in purses. Bradley was generous with his winnings. In fact, there was hardly a charity he didn't support. After the 1928 hurricane, he made large contributions to the Red Cross and to several churches for reconstruction, including one at which the pastor regularly denounced him from the pulpit. A devout Catholic, he contributed most of the money for the construction of St. Edward's Church. He helped build Good Samaritan and St. Mary's Hospitals. He would explain his generosity by saying he might as well dispose of his money while he was alive: "There are no pockets in a shroud."

Bradley had been a lot of things in the years before he followed Henry Flagler's railroad south into Florida, including ill. As a matter of fact, it was illness that led him into the horse business. Bradley was born on December 12, 1859, in Johnstown, Pennsylvania. He followed his father into the steel mills at age thirteen and later headed into the Wild West, where details of his life become vague. He handled mules, herded cows, washed dishes, mined, and prospected. Later, he would say he was Indian scout for General Nelson Miles and was present when Miles negotiated the surrender of Geronimo.

Edward Riley Bradley.
(The Palm Beach Post)

The West taught him about horses and also about gambling, one of the three most popular pastimes in mining camps. He evidently profited from his skills, a subject about which he was reticent. At any rate, by the time he started bookmaking at horse tracks in Memphis, Tennessee, and Hot Springs, Arkansas, he was a man of means. After losing money at the tracks, recouping it with a casino venture in El Paso, and marrying Agnes C. Curry of St. Louis, he popped up in Chicago in the late 1880s and quickly built up his fortune. He bought a hotel and subsequently invested in a clothing store and a casino. At other times (the chronology is unclear), he operated casinos in New Orleans, Louisville, and Indiana. Each was called The Bacchus Club.

But his busy schedule came to a halt in 1890, when he had a heart attack. His doctor advised a change of scenery, preferably to a rural area. Bradley decided on the Bluegrass Country of Kentucky and bought a tract near Lexington on which he established Idle Hour Farm. The shock of the heart attack and the easier pace of life in Kentucky seem to have molded the dignified, unruffled Bradley of later years. Not that he turned his back on gambling. He still was involved in bookmaking, and he backed casinos in Rockaway, New York, and Long Branch, New Jersey.

When Bradley heard of the new land Flagler had opened up on the east coast of Florida, he headed south for a look and soon started visiting St. Augustine. The possibilities of gambling in such affluent settings were obvious, so he and his brother, John, opened yet another Bacchus Club in 1891. When Flagler moved south to Palm Beach, the Bradleys followed. On today's Bradley Park, which then was alongside the railroad spur leading to Flagler's Royal Poinciana and Breakers Hotels, the brothers built an unpretentious, rambling wooden building with gray-shingled sides. It was painted white with green trim, Edward's racing colors. In 1898, the Beach Club opened for business. The name, incidentally, supposedly came from a portrait hanging inside the club of a gambler named Beach.

It has often been said that Flagler encouraged the Bradleys to open their Florida casinos to give his hotel guests some form of entertainment. Flagler expressed a different attitude in a June 9, 1898, letter to E. N. Dimick, a Palm Beach pioneer who had built the town's first hotel, the Coconut Grove House. Flagler said he didn't know the Bradleys' club was going to be used for gambling until after it had opened and that he had told Edward that he "should spare no pains or expense to compel him to stop the gambling. . . . I do know that gambling will drive away the better class of people, and encourage a class that none of us want, and I state here, most emphatically, that if the Club House cannot be closed peaceably or legally, I will close the two hotels, for I am determined that I will not furnish the grist for Mr. Bradley's gambling mill."

A couple of observations seem in order. First, Flagler did not close his hotels, despite his protestations, and the Bradleys did not close their casino. Second, it seems inconceivable that Flagler did not know the purpose of the club, considering he knew about the Bacchus operation in St. Augustine. It seems more likely that

Flagler's attitude toward the casinos was one of benign neglect and that the letter to Dimick was more about image than about substance.

Whatever the case, poor business almost shut the club down before it ever got off the ground. The problem, it turned out, was the "men only" rule. Wealthy women, who could not attend, were encouraging their husbands to stay away also. The club restaurant had a fairly good trade, but that was more of a hindrance than a help because it was a money-loser set up to attract gamblers. Near the end of the initial season, John prevailed over brother Edward's reluctance to allow both sexes, and women were admitted. From then on, the Beach Club never lost money.

How did the Beach Club remain in operation for more than four decades even though casino gambling was illegal? Officially, of course, it was not a casino. The articles of incorporation said it had been organized "for social purposes," including "such games or amusements as the management . . . and its members may from time to time agree upon." A state investigator once made an unannounced visit, but, thanks to a tip, the gambling equipment had been safely stored in a back room.

Beyond that, local people regarded the Beach Club as a tourist attraction more than anything else. They did not patronize it, and those from out of town who did go there also spent money elsewhere in the community. If all else failed, Bradley knew how to defend himself. The 1930s Senate inquiry supposedly came to naught after Bradley reminded one of the committee members, Huey Long of Louisiana, how much Bradley had helped Long's campaigns financially.

Besides, gambling in southeast Florida always had been fairly wide open. There were casinos in Broward County. Both bookmaking and a variation on the numbers racket known as bolita were common. After the Beach Club closed in 1945, much of its equipment was sent to the posh Lake Shore Club in Hypoluxo. It was used there until 1950 when another Senate inquiry, this one headed by Estes Kefauver of Tennessee, finally shut down the casino industry.

The Beach Club building was unpretentious. Its only identification was a pair of Old English letters, B. C., on the frosted glass that filled the upper part of the main door. Inside was a small, white-paneled reception room in which the club secretary handled applications for membership. According to Thomas "Tip" Reese, longtime secretary, the main requirements were "plenty of money and no squawks at losing." Those who passed muster went through another door into a hall that led to the restaurant and the ballroom, as the gambling room was euphemistically called. The decor, all in green and white, bespoke simple elegance.

Millions of dollars might be bet in the course of an evening, much of it on paper rather than in actual cash on the table. Despite this show of wealth, though, there was never an attempt to hold up the club. Perhaps would-be robbers observed that the doors were too narrow to allow a group of men to storm the building. Perhaps they knew that behind a latticework gallery overlooking the ballroom sat a sharpshooter with a loaded rifle. Perhaps they had heard that eighteen Pinkerton guards were among those employed.

The employees, all nonresidents, were sworn to secrecy as to what went on within the walls. They even were housed on the premises, in a plain wing of the building known as "the barracks." Edward Bradley also was near at hand; his home was connected to the north end of the building. Regardless of this secrecy, enough stories have leaked out to start a number of legends.

For instance, the seven o'clock dress rule became a problem one day when automaker Walter P. Chrysler, inadequately dressed for the evening, was down several thousand dollars as the deadline approached. When told of the time, he protested and said he wanted a chance to get even. The dapper Bradley—always dressed impeccably, up to a high, stiff collar—proposed they flip a coin, double or nothing. As Bradley flipped, Chrysler called "Heads!" Bradley caught the coin and, without looking, said, "You win, Walter." He had preserved the rules with grace, at a four-figure price.

The most famous story, however, concerns a woman who came to Bradley in tears one night and said her husband had lost all the money they had, five thousand dollars. Bradley was moved and gave her five one-thousand-dollar bills "on condition you promise me neither you nor your husband will ever enter the club again." The next night, as he was making his rounds at the tables, he spotted the young man the woman had pointed out as her husband. He immediately called the man into his office and began berating him:

"You were told never to come here again. You cannot afford that kind of money. Your wife agreed."

"My what?"

"Your wife."

"Colonel Bradley, I am not married. As for not affording it, I think I can. My name is Russell Firestone. I think you know my father, Harvey Firestone [founder of the tire company]."

Asked later what he did, Bradley would smile and say, "I didn't do anything. Any girl who can get the best of a tough old goat like me is welcome to five thousand dollars."

In the words of *The New York Times*, the Beach Club survived "all changes of administration, all reform waves, and had the support of the society leaders and industrial giants who made Palm Beach their winter home." What finally did it in was Bradley's failing health. In 1937, the aging widower—Mrs. Bradley had died in 1926—had a second heart attack. More followed over the next eight years, and in 1945, he sold the Beach Club. The end came in the early morning hours of August 15, 1946, at Idle Hour Farm. The following week, he was buried in Lexington.

Sources for this chapter include "No Run-of-the-Millionaires Here" by Cleveland Amory; "Colossus of Sporting World Holdover from More Spacious Times" by Robert Sullivan; *The Life and Career of Edward R. Bradley* by Thomas M. Cunningham; "Col. E. R. Bradley, Turf Leader, Dies" (obituary); and various letters, articles, and books included in the Theodore Pratt collection at Florida Atlantic University.

Chapter 10
Linton and Boynton
Cities on the Canal

Two politicians from Michigan gave their names to settlements that sprang up south of Lake Worth in the wake of Henry Flagler's railway. One name was changed almost immediately; the other endures.

After United States Representative William Seelye Linton of Saginaw, Michigan, heard about the opportunities on the new Florida frontier, he persuaded a friend, David Swinton, to go south with him early in 1895. In West Palm Beach, then the end of the railroad, they learned that there was land for sale to the south and headed that way by boat, first on Lake Worth and then on the newly dug Florida East Coast Canal (predecessor of today's Intracoastal Waterway). Linton liked what he saw and, with some financial aid from Swinton, arranged to purchase much of what now constitutes the central sections of Delray Beach and Boynton Beach. He hurried back to Michigan to sign up settlers.

It was a task virtually foreordained for success, because Linton was the sort of person who could talk people into seeing things his way. Cecil W. and Margoann Farrar characterize him as "an inveterate adventurer and promoter par excellence" in their book, *Incomparable Delray Beach—Its Early Life and Lore.*

Linton was born in St. Clair, Michigan, on February 4, 1856. He was still in his early twenties when he served two terms on the Bay County Board of Supervisors. In 1878, he married Ida M. Lowry and settled in the Saginaw area, where he joined the family lumber and salt businesses. But Linton also continued in public service, serving on the East Saginaw Common Council from 1883 to 1887 and in the Michigan House of Representatives the next two years. In 1890, he ran unsuccessfully for lieutenant governor on the Republican ticket. Two years later, he was elected to both the United States House of Representatives and the mayoralty of consolidated Saginaw. (He had sponsored the consolidation legislation.) Then, he decided to look south.

By the fall of 1895, Linton had rounded up eight settlers to return with him to Florida: E. Burslein Thomson, W. W. Blackmer,

Frank W. Chapman, Fason Baker, Peter Leurs, Otto Schroder, Kemp Burton, and Adolph Hofman. The Miami extension of Flagler's railroad was under way but not yet ready, so the last leg of the trip was once again by water. The only building in the area, the Orange Grove House of Refuge for shipwrecked sailors, was on the beach at a point now about a thousand feet north of Atlantic Avenue in Delray Beach. Keeper Stephen N. Andrews, one of the men from whom Linton had bought land, took in the settlers until they could build shelters on the five-acre tracts they had bought from Linton.

The town Linton had planned extended, in today's terms, from North Fourth Street to South Fourth Street and from the ocean west to West Eighth Avenue. By the end of that first year, the palmetto growth had been cleared from the fertile canal banks, and crops had been planted. Some of the pioneers even had sent for their families. Henry Sterling had set up the first store, and the Linton post office had been authorized. The following spring, the railroad was in operation, providing a means for shipping produce to market. Linton named the east-west division street for his friend Swinton, who apparently never revisited the area after that first journey in 1895. The freshwater lake west of town was given Mrs. Linton's first name.

The precise relationship between Linton and Nathan Smith Boynton has never been clear, but they probably knew each other. Boynton had been the most prominent figure in the various

William Seelye Linton.
(Delray Beach Historical Society Archives)

Nathan Smith Boynton.
(Boynton Beach Public Library)

Maccabee fraternal-beneficial organizations in Michigan, in which Linton also was active; both had been involved in politics; and both were from the same general area. In 1897, Boynton bought the northern portion of Linton's holdings. Boynton, however, was not interested in Florida land promotion, and by 1898, most of his land had gone back to Fred S. Dewey, from whom Linton had bought.

The land Boynton kept was the oceanfront tract homesteaded in 1879 by another Michigan man, whose name is spelled both "Hubel" and "Hubble." The homesteader had become tired of life in the wilderness after only a year and had let Andrews take over his claim. From Andrews, it went to Linton and then to Boynton, who built the Boynton Beach Hotel at the point where Ocean Avenue would reach the beach if it extended east of State Road A1A.

For a man prominent in two states, and after whom a whole city is named, Boynton remains somewhat of a mystery. He was relatively aloof—even considered by some to be unfriendly—although those few who knew him found him personable. He was born on June 23, 1837, in Port Huron, Michigan, the city where he spent most of his life. He entered the mercantile business in 1856, only to go broke in the panic of the following year. So he hit the road and wound up in Cincinnati, where he married German-born Annie Fieldei in 1858.

When the Civil War broke out, Boynton returned to Port Huron and enlisted. He was a first lieutenant before leaving the state and a major by war's end. He was in campaigns all along the western front, and was one of the first Union soldiers to enter Atlanta. Once a Democrat, Boynton became active in Republican politics after the war because of his opposition to slavery. Following the panic of 1873, he turned to the Greenback, a precursor of the Progressive movement that advocated a freer money policy. His only subsequent public office was as mayor of Port Huron in 1874–1875 and again in 1894.

Between those terms, much of Boynton's energy was consumed heading the various groups known as Maccabees. During the two decades of internecine fighting, he was generally allied with those forces urging conservative policies in management of the group's funds. Boynton had fought a lot of battles, and had lost quite a few of them, by the time he bought his Florida land. Possibly, he was becoming embittered.

Linton was having his problems, too. By 1897, it appeared his land promotion had run into financial trouble. Perhaps the reason he sold some of his holdings to Boynton was to raise money. Frost, crop failure and the general difficulties of frontier life were taking their toll. New farmers stopped arriving, and old ones began to return north. By 1898, Linton was far behind in his payments on the land. Creditors moved to collect from the settlers, many of whom were under the impression that Linton had held clear title when he sold them the land. Sterling later said he wound up paying for his property twice. This turn of events sent more settlers north and hurt the reputation of Linton, who had returned to Michigan after founding the community. On November 19, 1898, the Linton post office was renamed after Blackmer's hometown of Delray, Michigan, then a suburb of Detroit and today part of the city.

The worst was over. The renamed community embarked on a period of slow, steady growth that made it into a town. The first public building was the 1897 schoolhouse, which was also used for church services and community meetings. The first hotel, called The Inn, was built in 1900. Another schoolhouse was built in 1901, the first church—Methodist—in 1902. The first physician, Dr. J. R. Cason Jr., arrived in 1905, and the first telephones were installed in 1908. By 1910, there were 250 residents, and they decided it was time to incorporate. The charter for the town of Delray was approved on September 4, 1911, and John Shaw Sundy was elected mayor with fifty-three of the fifty-six votes cast.

To the north, Boynton was experiencing a parallel development. Dewey had filed his plat on September 29, 1898, and was selling farmland, giving a lot in the new town with each farm sold. Many of the workers on Boynton's hotel decided to buy and become farmers. Boynton even did a bit of farming himself, putting in a citrus grove west of the hotel.

The living was not exactly ideal, though. Subtropical climate means mild winters, but it also means plenty of mosquitoes. Mosquitoes remained a major hindrance until large-scale drainage and spraying after World War II. Glen Murray, a member of one of Boynton's first families, remembered eighty years later the misery of his first night at his new home, trying to sleep in a tent in the middle of a swamp. The environment, combined with the lack of sanitation facilities, spawned disease as well as discomfort. Cattle ticks were so bad that many pioneers subsisted on canned milk, and death from typhoid fever was an ever-present possibility. And then there were the snakes.

The Bijou, Delray Beach's first movie house, at West Atlantic and First Avenues.
(The Palm Beach Post)

None of that, however, was enough to keep new settlers from the cheap farmland and comfortable climate. By 1900, Boynton had its first school. The first church, again Methodist, was established in 1905. The settlers here, however, were not as anxious to incorporate as were those in Delray. It was not until 1920 that the town of Boynton was chartered, with G. E. Coon as first mayor.

The area's farming could be characterized as truck farming without the trucks. It never was a subsistence agriculture; the farmers grew cash crops and bought supplies. A variety of vegetables were grown at first, but after the turn of the century, pineapple steadily became more popular because it thrived in soil too sandy for other crops. Pineapple remained the dominant crop in the area until forced out by competition from low-cost Cuban pineapple shipped over Flagler's railroad from Key West.

Once the communities were under way, their founders were nearly forgotten. Linton never returned, and Boynton came in town only during the winter, when he stayed at his hotel and generally kept to himself. Most of his friends in Boynton were friends from Michigan who wintered with him. Boynton died on May 27, 1911, shortly after his seasonal return to Port Huron.

Linton's fiasco in Florida didn't damage his name too severely. He was defeated for reelection to Congress in 1896, but he was appointed postmaster of Saginaw in 1898 by President William McKinley. He served in that job—traveling to Europe, Asia, and Africa to study overseas postal systems—until 1914, when he sought unsuccessfully the Republican nomination for governor of Michigan. Later, as president of the Saginaw Board of Trade, he presided over projects that "have transformed dilapidated property, jungle and tangle, bog and mire, into useful fine scenic parks, places of recreation and enjoyment for all," in the words of the book *History of Saginaw County*.

In 1919, Linton was appointed to the state Tax Commission and was its secretary when stricken by a heart attack late in 1927. On November 22, he died in Lansing, long famous in Michigan and virtually forgotten in what by then was the city of Delray Beach. (The town of Delray had merged in 1927 with the town of Delray Beach, which had been formed in 1923 along the ocean.) In the city Linton founded, today his name is merely a boulevard.

This chapter was compiled from documents provided by the Saginaw County Historical Society and the Bentley Historical Library. Additional information comes from *Incomparable Delray Beach—Its Early Life and Lore* by Cecil W. and Margoann Farrar and *Information for Homeseekers* (anonymous pamphlet).

Chapter 11
George Morikami
Making His Way in a New Land

They came from halfway around the world in search of land and prosperity. Most of them found neither. Now, all are gone. Only a park west of Delray Beach and a street in Boca Raton mark the passage of the Japanese settlement of Yamato.

As the twentieth century began, the profitability of pineapple agriculture in southeast Florida was becoming evident. The hardy pineapple could be grown on land too dry and sandy for other crops; it shipped well; and it brought a good price. But pineapple growing required a lot of labor. A young Japanese entrepreneur named Joseph Sakai dreamed of a syndicate of Florida farming colonies manned by countrymen. The dream and the opportunity met at Yamato, with the Florida East Coast Railway furnishing both advice and materials on the condition that the farmers ship by rail.

The farmers were recruited both from those Japanese left unemployed in the United States by the end of the great railroad-building era and from those left destitute in Japan by the Russo-Japanese War of 1905, which was a military success but an economic disaster. One of the young men who disembarked from an FEC train that summer day in 1906 was George Morikami. Unlike most of the others recruited from Japan, he was a first son and, as such, would inherit his father's small farm near the old Japanese capital of Kyoto. But, even with this land, his family was poor, and the five hundred dollars he had been promised for two years of work in Florida was a lot of money.

Yamato was several miles north of another small pineapple-farming community named Boca Raton, which after World War II would grow to absorb Yamato and everything in between. Unlike Yamato, Boca Raton was an old name in Florida. The inlet is found on maps dating to the sixteenth century, often misnamed or incorrectly located but there nonetheless. The words have been translated as "Rat's Mouth," from its shape on a map, or "Place of Hidden Rocks," both of which have their champions and their detractors.

As was true of much of southeast Florida, Boca Raton was not considered suitable for settlement until Henry Flagler brought his FEC Railway through. In 1896—the year the rails went in—T. M. Rickards, a civil engineer in Flagler's employ, came to the area aboard a schooner and liked what he saw. He returned the following year and built a driftwood home on the Intracoastal Waterway (then privately owned and called the Florida East Coast Canal), just south of today's Palmetto Park Road. Rickards surveyed and subdivided about five hundred acres and sold the pieces in ten-acre tracts at twenty dollars an acre. Most of the land was planted with pineapple under his supervision, and the community of Boca Raton was born.

These settlers were doing just fine, so there seemed to be no reason that the Japanese shouldn't do as well. One reason soon surfaced, however: a lack of capital. The Yamato operation was bankrupt within eighteen months. There would be no five hundred dollars for Morikami, nor for anyone else. "I looked, and I had no money," he told an interviewer near the end of his life. "Not even enough to go back home on. So I had to stay here. I have never been back."

Many of those who could afford the passage returned to Japan. Many others went elsewhere in the United States. A few remained at Yamato, a Japanese word that means "great peaceful land" and is the name of a clan that ruled Japan in the fourth century. Morikami went to New York City, Chicago, even Vancouver, Canada, in search of work, with no success. In 1909, he was in Eau Gallie (now part of Melbourne), where he attended first grade to learn English. The slim young man, by now in his early twenties, got "excellent" marks in arithmetic, geography, grammar, history, reading, spelling, and writing.

Morikami began farming to the north of Yamato, in what today is the Old Germantown Road area. By that time, Yamato had become even smaller. The collapse of the Florida pineapple industry brought on by Cuban competition had forced more of the Japanese out. One of those who had remained was Sakai, supposedly of noble lineage and apparently the acknowledged leader of the community.

Despite the financial reverses suffered by his countrymen, Morikami planted pineapple, for he was a determined man, willing to invest the labor required and still sell his fruit at a competitive price. By 1915, he had earned enough to buy his own land in Yamato. He could have gone back to Japan then, but he seemed genuinely in love with his new land, a love he would show in many ways in the decades to come, including donating land for a large county park.

Financially, his course generally improved, though not without some reverses. He almost died from an ulcer once, and the medical expenses set him back greatly. The Depression, of course, was another low point. By the late 1930s, "I had a few acres—a small-scale farm," he said. "I was hardly making things do. Then a storm came and washed out my crop." He sought a bank loan to recoup his losses, but just about that time, the bombing of Pearl Harbor put the United States at war

George Morikami.
(Morikami Museum)

with Morikami's native land. Needless to say, he didn't get the loan.

That was not all. The army took his land in Yamato to use as part of its Boca Raton air base, and he became a semiprisoner in the country in which he had lived for thirty-five years. Though Morikami was not interned, as were Japanese-Americans in California, he was not fully free, either. "George had a guardian . . . all during the war," said Sadie Sundy, a Delray Beach pioneer, in an interview for the University of Florida Oral History project. "He couldn't even sign his checks."

It was then that he started buying up land west of Military Trail, in the Kings Point area of suburban Delray Beach. The legal restrictions did not affect his relations with other residents, who were united in their praise of his industriousness. In fact, it is said in one story, perhaps apocryphal, that neighbors once surrounded his house to intimidate—successfully—federal agents who had come to question him.

"I kept buying land," Morikami told Drs. George E. Pozzetta and Harry A. Kersey Jr. of Florida Atlantic University in another Oral History project interview. "I don't know why I did it. Whenever I see good land, I want it, whether I need it or not. The price was fifteen dollars [an acre] to start . . . and gradually going up." By 1943, he owned several hundred acres. Never again would he seek a bank loan. "When I was dead broke and I needed the money, the bank wouldn't lend it to me," he said in 1974. "Now they would lend me whatever I ask. But I have never borrowed one cent from them."

In addition to pineapples, Morikami grew tomatoes and bananas, making substantial profits on all of them. As his holdings increased, he had to hire labor, but he continued to do as much of the work as possible himself. Even in his later years, he often would dig the ground for pineapples with his bare hands, saying that only he knew how to do it properly.

Though he never saw his family or his home village again, he periodically sent money to his relatives, including a sister and her three children. Ross Snyder, a friend of Morikami's, believes Morikami wasn't sure his entry into the United States had been legal and was afraid of being denied reentry if he left the country.

Morikami never married, though he once came close, according to Snyder. In the 1920s, he corresponded with a German woman whose father was a New York City policeman. They became engaged, and Morikami built a house in the Germantown Road area. But she suddenly fell ill with pneumonia and died before she could come to Boca Raton.

Despite his wealth—his land was valued at more than one million dollars in later years—he lived in a drab yellow trailer perched atop a levee he had built and named Mount Fuji. "I like this," Morikami explained. "It is simple. The land is all around me. I eat fresh fruits and vegetables I grow myself. No meat. I eat when I am hungry, day or night. If I had to live in town, I couldn't have this."

He showed his attachment to his new nation in various ways. For one, he refused to speak Japanese, even though he still was fluent. When asked a question in Japanese, he would answer in English. And when Morikami cut back his operations as he grew older, he gave away the land he no longer used. In the mid-1960s, he gave the state forty acres for an agricultural experimental station. In 1973, he gave another forty acres to the county, which officials developed into Morikami Park and a museum focusing on Japanese history and culture. After donating ninety more acres to the park in 1975, he had about fifteen acres left for himself.

Even as he neared his ninetieth birthday, he continued to farm. He would rise about seven o'clock in the morning and would work three hours. The night of February 28, 1976, Morikami became quite ill.

The Morikami Museum, built on land donated by George Morikami.
(The Palm Beach Post)

According to longtime friend Art Pickering, he didn't want medical help. Pickering left him alone about two in the morning. Five hours later, when Pickering returned, Morikami was dead. "He died the way he wanted to," Pickering said. "No hospitals or doctors shooting dope into him to keep his heart pumping."

With Morikami's death, the story of Yamato was over.

Sources for this chapter include the monograph "Yamato Colony: A Japanese Presence in South Florida" by George E. Pozzetta, Ph. D., and Harry A. Kersey Jr., Ph. D., as well as the interview on which that monograph was based. Additional information comes from "Farming Lures Early Settlers to Boca Raton" by Pat Curry; an anonymous article in *Fiesta* magazine; and a telephone interview with Ross Snyder.

Chapter 12
Thomas Leroy Jefferson
Son of Slavery, Healer

The Palm Beach Post Office and the Paramount Center frame a two-block stretch of North County Road that houses shops for the well-to-do. Nothing about the area suggests that a century ago it was a collection of palmetto and driftwood shacks that constituted a pioneer African-American community. Known as the Styx, the area was home to those who had come to help build Henry M. Flagler's railroad, until land values made it profitable to relocate these squatters west of the lake.

When they were healthy, the members of this society worked in and around Flagler's Palm Beach hotels, the Royal Poinciana and the original Breakers. When they were ill, they visited a lean, quiet healer named Dr. Thomas Leroy Jefferson. His story is intertwined with the story of this African-American community, as it was pushed steadily westward until consolidating into what today is considered to be its "historic" core in northwestern West Palm Beach.

For four decades, interrupted by a brief retirement cut short by the Depression, Jefferson practiced medicine and operated a drug store. He was born in Hazlehurst, Mississippi, in 1867; two years earlier, he would have come into the world a slave. His father, "Uncle Tom" Jefferson, was so light-skinned that he lived as a white man after Emancipation, becoming a major cotton grower and a leading citizen of Hazlehurst, even though his slave origins were known. There is a family legend that he was related to the nation's third president through Sally Hemmings, one of the president's slaves, possibly explaining his acceptance by the town. Historian Fawn Brodie believed that Hemmings bore President Jefferson several children, but other historians disagree.

One of the elder Jefferson's daughters also chose to live as white, but his son Thomas Leroy wanted to be known as an African-American. Holding to this idea, he became a teacher and drug-store operator in New Iberia, Louisiana, where he met and wed Georgia Broussard. Soon afterward, he set his sights on a medical education.

Thomas Leroy Jefferson.
(Palm Beach Community College)

For an African-American in the late nineteenth century, that meant attending Meharry Medical School, established in 1867 in Nashville. After earning his degree, he moved to Orange, Texas, then New Orleans, where his daughter Maude Kay was born. By 1900, the family had come to Palm Beach.

Early on, the Styx was the best-known African-American community in the Palm Beaches, but its residents were not the first of their race in the area. Eleven slaves were shipwrecked with Jonathan Dickinson in 1696. And other slaves undoubtedly fled south in the eighteenth and early nineteenth centuries to take refuge with Seminole Indians. Early in 1843, William Henry Peck brought several slaves with him when he came to help his father establish a homestead in the Susanna settlement (near today's Fort Pierce). Though the Pecks abandoned their claim just two years later, it is likely—but not certain—that other Indian River settlers brought slaves with them, too.

There would not be any other known African-American residents of the Palm Beaches or south Indian River for another four decades, but in 1890, they were present in at least three areas on the shores of Lake Worth. The first to arrive apparently was Will Melton, who was reported to be in the area in 1885 and who in 1888 purchased about six and a half acres of land near the Oak Lawn Hotel, in what the next year would become Riviera. Other nearby early African-American settlers included the families of Jake Gildersleeve, Ed Cain, and Thomas Taylor. By 1892, one African-American church had been built, and in 1894, a second was being organized.

The 1890 residents of what would become Palm Beach in the Flagler era included at least six African-Americans: Rich Carleton and his wife; General Kelly; Millie Smith; and Henry and Tom Speed. Henry Speed later prospered in real estate and construction. When Flagler first visited the island, he arrived on a boat piloted by George Williams, who stayed on and became a popular pilot with yacht owners.

To the south, the federal government granted Samuel and Fannie James a patent in 1890 for what would become the southeast portion of the city of Lake Worth. They built a home on what now are the two city blocks bounded by Second and Fourth Avenues and J and K Streets and apparently kept title to their land until 1912, despite Fannie's semiprotest against the government, a story featured in a historical talk presented at the city's now-defunct Fiesta del Sol (Festival of the Sun):

> When the government approved the patent request, the first post office was established in Lake Worth. It was registered as the town of Jewell, as this area was known. The small cottage that housed the post office was located near the lake, in the vicinity of what now is Lake Avenue. Fannie was named postmistress and took care of the office for some time, though the exact tenure of her office is unknown.
>
> One day, for some reason, Fannie got disgusted and sent her resignation to Washington. Either because the officials there failed to reply or were not as prompt as she thought they should have been, Fannie picked up all the mail, including the sign, and dumped them in the lake.
>
> Thus ended the first post office in Lake Worth.

To the south, among the African-Americans listed as prominent in the Delray Beach of a century ago, according to authors Cecil W. and Margoann Farrar, were Joseph Baldwin, James Freeman, George Green, Joseph Green, Reverend Joseph Hanna, Charlie Miller, Jesse Nelson, Mary Nesbit, Emma Reynolds, and families with surnames Ivy, Jackson, and Youngblood.

The coming of Flagler's railroad increased African-American settlement in three ways. First, construction required a lot of workmen, most of whom were African-American. Second, the rails set off a boom in farming. The most important early crop, pineapple, required a lot of field labor, usually supplied by African-Americans. To this day, many of the communities with the largest percentages of African-Americans—Fort Pierce, Stuart, Boynton Beach, Delray Beach, Belle Glade, and Pahokee—are those that originated entirely or largely as farming communities. And finally, African-Americans were needed to build, maintain, and staff the tourist facilities Flagler was building on Palm Beach.

To serve this growing group of African-Americans, Jefferson set up his first medical office in the area, in the Styx. But he would not be there for long. The resort community was growing, and the owners of the land on which the African-Americans were squatting soon wanted to develop it. There are various versions of how the Styx actually changed hands. According to one story, Flagler invited the residents to a party in West Palm Beach to get them out of the way while their homes were burned. A less dramatic, and more likely, version tells of a gradual exodus during the first decade of the new century.

Most Styx residents apparently moved into the area bounded by North Dixie Highway (then Poinsettia Avenue), the FEC Railway, and Fifteenth and Twenty-third Streets, forming the Pleasant City community of West Palm Beach. Others, including Jefferson, relocated into an area to the south where African-Americans already were living. By 1911, Jefferson had an office in a frame building on North Olive Avenue (across from where the city parking garage now stands). The tall, lean physician was a familiar sight in downtown, pedaling his bicycle to work while puffing on one of his ever-present cigars.

At that time, the racial dividing line in West Palm Beach was Clematis Street. Banyan Street was lined with businesses owned by African-Americans. Noah Wilson, who lived for two years on the one hundred block of North Narcissus Avenue, said that a few African-Americans were still living on Root Trail in Palm Beach when he arrived in 1911, but that the last of them—except for live-in servants—had moved across the lake by 1912.

That would not be the last move. As West Palm Beach increased in size, whites coveted the east-side business property occupied by African-Americans. Carl Robinson, Jefferson's son-in-law, recalled the doctor's account: "Blacks were promised if they would agree to move their businesses [west] across the [Florida East Coast] railroad tracks, that whites would not come over there and [set up] business. . . . About 1924 or 1925, an ordinance was passed prohibiting whites from coming across the tracks [with businesses], and that stuck up for a long time, up until about 1960. It was segregation, but it was in our favor and we didn't kick." Robinson, who operated several grocery stores at one time or another, noted that the ordinance protected smaller African-American businesses from competition with the larger white-owned businesses.

With whites south of Clematis Street and east of the tracks and a shallow lake in the low-lying area west of the ridge where the rail station now stands, the only way the African-American neighborhood could expand was to the north. It gradually spread before and during the 1920's boom until it reached Twenty-third Street, where it was cut off again, this time by the growth of Northwood Hills, which then was all-white.

To make sure people knew whose neighborhood was whose, the city changed the names of Sapodilla and Rosemary Avenues between Clematis Street and Okeechobee Boulevard to Georgia and Florida Avenues, respectively. This is another distinction that was blurred when the African-American neighborhood expanded south of Clematis after 1970. The original names have now been restored.

Throughout these times of change, Jefferson remained a respected member of the community, not only because of his knowledge but also his personality. His son-in-law described him as "quiet . . . not a mixer," the sort of person who inspires confidence by his carriage. And if there was one thing in which he didn't believe, it was debt. "If he bought an automobile, he paid cash for it," Robinson said. "He would put so much in savings every night for vacation the next year. When he died, he owed thirty-five cents, and that was for a week's laundry."

At sixty, Jefferson decided to retire. That lasted only two years, until the 1929 stock-market crash took everything he had but his property. Undaunted, he picked up his medical satchel and declared, "I can always make a living at this." He continued to do just that until a couple of years before his death on September 29, 1939.

The seventy-two years of Jefferson's life almost precisely cover the era from Emancipation to the beginning of the modern Civil Rights movement, which got much of its impetus from the egalitarianism of the World War II era, though most whites were not aware anything was changing until school segregation was outlawed in 1954. He was a son of slavery and a father of the contemporary African-American, both spiritually and temporally.

Biographical information for this chapter came from an interview with Carl Robinson. Other sources include "The Indian River Settlement: 1842-1849" by Joseph D. Cushman Jr.; *A History of Riviera Beach, Florida* by Lynn Brink; *Incomparable Delray Beach—Its Early Life and Lore* by Cecil W. and Margoann Farrar; and an interview with Noah Wilson.

Chapter 13

Hugh deLausset Willoughby
Farther, Faster, Higher

Hugh deLausset Willoughby liked to be first wherever he went, whether it was across a jumping pit or through the Everglades, along the beach or in the air. A list of his firsts, culled from family documents in the Martin County Historical Society files at Elliott Museum, would fill a good-sized obelisk. While he still was a youth, he brought the bicycle and dry-plate photography to the United States. At the University of Pennsylvania, he became the school's first letterman. By 1894, he was experimenting with aviation.

He was the first person known to cross the Everglades from Harney River to Miami, the first to drive an automobile from Philadelphia to Jacksonville, and the first to construct a biplane with propellers that pulled rather than pushed. He drove in the first auto race on the beach at Ormond, organized the Naval Reserve in Rhode Island, and owned the first yacht with a wireless telegraph. He had the first speedboat with an automobile-type engine, made the first aerial photographs of Philadelphia and Miami, and participated on two continents in ballooning, which he considered to be the king of sports. He held fourteen aviation patents and a fifteenth for an improved deep-sea fishing leader. His system of front-and-rear elevators, coordinated to improve vertical maneuvering, was used by both Orville Wright—whom Willoughby assisted on his first flight over Washington, D.C., in 1908—and by Glenn Curtiss.

Willoughby was born on August 7, 1856, in Delaware County, New York. When he was fourteen, his father took him to Paris. There, he watched Ernest Michaux tinker with a two-wheeled contraption known as a boneshaker due to the quality of its ride. His father told him he could have one if he learned to ride it. He did, and thus the bicycle came to the United States. The teenager also brought a new form of photography across the Atlantic. It was a process one of his teachers in Paris had developed using dry plates rather than the wet ones that had been used since the time of Daguerre.

Willoughby graduated from the University of Pennsylvania in 1877 as a mining and geological engineer. Along the way, he played on the school's first football team, rowed, and starred in track and field. He won the long jump at the first Intercollegiate Athletic Association meet in 1876, thus becoming the first person entitled to wear the Penn letter. Willoughby never seemed to use his degree; then again, he didn't have to since his family was wealthy. He had picked up an interest in ballooning in Paris and had started racing yachts when he graduated from Penn. The development of the internal combustion engine would open yet another avenue.

Willoughby first saw South Florida on a fishing trip in 1877 and returned virtually every winter thereafter. After a number of years in Palm Beach on his houseboat, *Manatee*, he bought a tract on Sewall's Point and spent his last thirty-two winters there, extolling the virtues of and working to improve the facilities of the Stuart area.

Perhaps his most lasting fame in Florida came from his Everglades trek of 1897. Entering the wilderness from Harney River (in the Ten Thousand Islands area), he and Ed Brewer, a veteran South Florida guide, spent fifteen days on a zigzag route before emerging in Miami. Along the way, they named a hammock for Willoughby, who told of the journey in a book entitled *Across the Everglades*, illustrated with his own photographs. In it, he dispelled a number of popular notions, in particular the idea that the Everglades was a swamp.

A lot of environmental problems would have been averted had public officials of the twentieth century recognized, as did Willoughby and Marjory Stoneman Douglas, author of *Everglades: River of Grass*, that the Everglades is, in fact, a river. "Pure water is running in it," Willoughby wrote, "and no stagnant pool can be found. In the daytime the

Hugh deLausset Willoughby at the tiller, 1900.
(Historical Society of Martin County)

cool breeze has an undisturbed sweep, and the water is protected from overheating by the shade the grass affords. Water plants of various kinds and several varieties of fish and reptiles keep the balance of life, as in a self-sustaining aquarium."

In 1896, Willoughby and Brewer had reconnoitered the area, accompanied by Willoughby's wife, Augusta, whom he had married in 1878, and their son, Hugh Jr. In addition to exploring the area, Willoughby established a survey line through the Everglades and collected specimens of plants and animals for the University of Pennsylvania. He also conducted a confidential survey of channels in the Ten Thousand Islands area for the Naval War College. Willoughby had obtained a reserve commission when he organized the Rhode Island Naval Reserve and had been activated in 1896. He was sent to the war college as part of the buildup for the war with Spain, a war that already was expected though it would not break out until 1898. He would escort a naval squadron south from Jacksonville to the Florida Keys.

The Willoughbys made Rhode Island their summer spot, building an expansive home known as The Chalet in Newport. Of course, Willoughby spent a lot of his time away setting records, such as the twenty-hour, fifteen-minute auto trip in 1903 from Philadelphia to Newport, a distance of 303 miles. Winters were spent in Florida, usually in Palm Beach, where he organized boating activities. In 1908, the New York Yacht Club—in which he held membership number two—decided to open a winter facility in Florida; Willoughby began looking for a site. Deciding that Miami and Palm Beach were not suitable, he traveled north to Sewall's Point, a narrow spit of land east of Stuart between the St. Lucie and Indian Rivers. The yacht club never did establish a winter home, but Willoughby did. He bought a tract from Henry E. Sewall, then the point's only resident, and constructed his palatial Mandalay.

The Stuart area was one of the few places Willoughby wasn't first. Given the fortunes of those first would-be settlers, that was just as well. James A. Hutchinson was killed in a storm before he could develop the island that bears his name, which he had received in an 1807 Spanish land grant. John M. Hanson and Eusebio M. Gomez, two other grant recipients, accomplished little. There may have been some Armed Occupation Act settlers in the area at one time, but the first known settlers, according to the Martin County Historical

Society's *History of Martin County*, were Mr. and Mrs. Frank Prescott, who arrived in 1878 by ox-drawn wagon over the remnants of the cross-state military road built during the Second Seminole War. They settled on a high cabbage-palm hammock about eleven and a half miles southwest of Stuart.

In January of 1879, Dr. James A. Henshall visited the area and described it in glowing terms to readers of his book *Camping and Cruising in Florida*. He said black-bass fishing in the south fork of the St. Lucie River "was really too much of a good thing. On favorable days, even with the artificial fly, one soon tired of the sport, for it required no skill whatsoever to lure them from the dark but clear water. . . . The black-bass fishing of the St. Lucie cannot be surpassed by anyplace in Florida or for that matter in the United States." As an aside, Henshall tells of visiting a hermit on Hutchinson Island who was called "Old Cuba." According to *History of Martin County*, this probably is the same man known to others as "Portugee Joe." He drowned a couple of years later.

About the same time, Thomas E. Richards and R. D. Hoke settled in the Eden area, along Indian River just north of today's St. Lucie County line. Within a couple of years, brothers Hubert and Willis Bessey had homesteaded part of what now is Stuart, and John L. Jensen was growing pineapple on the low hills of the area that still bears his name. In 1881, that area had a post office named Waveland. Other settlers trickled in during the next thirteen years, but the area still was relatively inaccessible until Flagler brought his railroad through in 1894 en route to Palm Beach.

Most affected by the transportation was the settlement of Potsdam, on the south shore of St. Lucie River. Trails to the early farmsteads radiated from the train station like spokes from a wheel. The station is now gone, but the spokes still are there, meeting at Confusion Corner. The settlers, looking for a new name for their settlements, decided on that of Homer T. Stuart, who purportedly was the black sheep of a prominent New England family and a specialist in fishing and drinking. Some said his name was chosen because he had a sign on a store that would easily transfer to the train station.

Meanwhile, Jupiter Island already was earning the image it retains to this day as a home for those too wealthy for Palm Beach. The Hobe Sound Yacht Club was organized in 1892. Among regular winter visitors was actor Joseph Jefferson. And an occasional guest both there

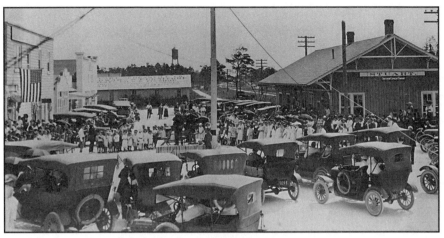

Downtown Stuart on Memorial Day, 1918.
(The Palm Beach Post)

and in Stuart was President Grover Cleveland, beginning a tradition that has continued through President Bill Clinton's visit to professional golfer Greg Norman in 1997.

At the turn of the century, the St. Lucie River divided Dade and Brevard Counties. Five years later, the area between the St. Lucie and Sebastian Rivers became St. Lucie County. In 1909, the year after Willoughby took up residence on Sewall's Point, the area from the river south to what today is Floranada Road in Fort Lauderdale became Palm Beach County. Stuart became the area's first incorporated city in 1914 and in 1925 became the seat of Martin County, named for Governor John W. Martin, who apparently appreciated the honor so much that he pushed the act creating the county through the legislature.

Willoughby got right to work promoting his new home. He formed the Sewall's Point Land Company, naming himself president and Henry E. Sewall vice president. They spent two hundred thousand dollars on docks, an inn, and ten miles of rock road. Lots sold fairly quickly at a good profit. Willoughby also continued to open frontiers and set more records. After assisting Wright with his Washington flight, Willoughby built his *War Hawk* in Atlantic City, New Jersey. Besides being the first biplane with forward propellers, it was the first plane that could be started by crank from the pilot's seat and the first to use Willoughby's twin-elevator design. In 1915, he was the first to demonstrate the dropping of a Whitehead torpedo from an airplane.

In 1928, at the age of seventy-one, Willoughby was the nation's oldest active pilot. He remained active until a hip injury in the mid-1930s for the most part confined him to his homes. In the spring of 1939, his up-and-down condition took a turn for the worse. Two weeks later, on April 4, he died at eighty-two.

Mandalay is gone, but the Willoughby name lives as that of a creek, a boulevard, and a development near Stuart and as a street in Brooklyn. It also lives in the spirit of those who throughout the ages have sought to go farther, faster, and higher.

Biographical information for this chapter comes from the files of the Martin County Historical Society. Other sources include *History of Martin County* by Janet Hutchinson and *Camping and Cruising in Florida* by James A. Henshall.

Chapter 14
Peter Raulerson
Cattle on the Big Lake

One day in 1896, Peter Raulerson decided he needed more room for his cattle, a decision that would be pivotal in the history of the savanna area immediately north of Lake Okeechobee. Raulerson drove his herd southeast from Basinger until he found land he liked, in the bend of Taylor Creek near the lake's north end. He stayed for the remaining fifty-one years of his life, a friend to everyone and founder of a dynasty.

At first, it seems a bit surprising that there was not one non-Indian settler on Lake Okeechobee as late as 1895. The area had been a cultural center for prehistoric Indians two thousand years before, and the lake was known to Spaniards who had cruised Florida's coasts just a quarter century after Columbus first sailed to the New World. After a closer look, however, it is a bit more understandable. The area was quite isolated: until the 1880s, there had been no dependable access for any watercraft larger than a canoe. And none of the land around the big lake was particularly suitable for cash crops; it took twentieth-century drainage to make farming along the southern shore possible.

Then there were the insects and the diseases. Consider a description in a letter written in February of 1856 by a visitor to the east coast but equally applicable to interior areas: "The mosquitoes fly for about five months during the year, commencing about the middle of May. You cannot work only just a little in the middle of the day. It's also pretty bad for fever and ague [a disease similar to malaria]. I have been sick with it ever since last October, but I am now getting over it."

None of these problems seems to have deterred the prehistoric Indians who lived at various sites around the lake as early as possibly 1000 B.C. In fact, a major ceremonial center was developed at Fisheating Creek in 500 B.C. and another at Belle Glade a millennium later. The prehistoric cultures eventually gave way to Seminole Indians, who in turn were reduced greatly in number during the three nineteenth-century Seminole Wars.

The outside world paid little attention to the Lake Okeechobee basin between the 1837 battle at Taylor Creek and the 1881 deal by which the state sold Hamilton Disston four million acres it had obtained from the federal government under the 1850 Swamp and Overflowed Lands Act. Disston agreed to pay twenty-five cents an acre, or one million dollars, most of which he raised by selling half the land to Sir Edward Reed for six hundred thousand dollars. Disston was also given 1,652,711 acres of state land, supposedly half of what he had drained, though, in fact, he had drained no more than fifty thousand acres.

Despite the title of this federal act, much of Disston's land was anything but swamp. Besides the area around Lake Okeechobee and the Caloosahatchee and Kissimmee Rivers, it included much of the ridge area and extended north almost to Orlando. Disston set up a camp at what would become the city of Kissimmee and put dredgers to work making his land accessible.

During the next decade, Disston began a number of projects, some of which failed and others that succeeded. Among his successes was a channel he opened from the Gulf of Mexico to Kissimmee via the Caloosahatchee River, Lake Okeechobee, and the Kissimmee River. The Panic of 1893 set Disston's work back, and in 1896, he committed suicide in Philadelphia. Besides the dredging, his accomplishments were few. Nevertheless, he drew attention to the area.

One witness was a cattleman named Peter Raulerson, who had come to Basinger (where U.S. 98 crosses the river northwest of Okeechobee) in 1874, at age seventeen. By the time Disston died, Raulerson's family was coming of age—his oldest son, Lewis, was fifteen—and he began to get restless. "He was a pioneer at heart," said his daughter, Faith Raulerson Meserve, "When a place began to get too thick, he had ideas of moving on."

The lure that drew him southeast was free land, state-owned property that any homesteader could use to graze cattle. Driving three yoke of oxen, he looked along the savanna until he came to the creek named for Zachary Taylor, the president-to-be who led soldiers there in the 1837 Battle of Okeechobee. Raulerson fenced off a 160-acre homestead and built a rambling, two-story log house near what is today South Parrott Avenue in Okeechobee city. As other settlers began to drift into the area, the Raulerson home became the unofficial community center.

So that his family could join him, Raulerson single-handedly set up a school system. Not only were the classes held in his home, but he also boarded the teacher sent from Titusville (today's Okeechobee County then was part of Brevard County) and the pupils, who were scattered from the Kissimmee River east to Taylor Creek. Raulerson paid half of the teacher's salary and provided wagon transportation for the students, picking them up Sunday afternoon and returning them Friday afternoon. While making the rounds, he delivered snuff to the homesteads.

Peter and Louisiana Raulerson.
(Okeechobee County Historical Society)

One of the early teachers, a vivacious, red-haired South Carolinian named Tantie Huckabee, gave her name to the post office when it was set up in 1902. Raulerson's wife, Louisiana Chandler Raulerson, operated the office out of a valise kept under a bed, receiving the mail twice a week from Fort Drum and handing it out to the settlers as they came by. In 1905, their son Lewis opened Tantie's first general store, a predecessor to the shoe and men's clothing store grandson Hiram operated until 1978 in downtown Okeechobee. Supplies were brought in from Fort Myers though the Disston canal. Later, Lewis succeeded his mother at the post office.

There was no government nearer than Fort Pierce (by now Tantie was in St. Lucie County). Peter was the acknowledged community leader, as well as the area's county commissioner. When Okeechobee city was incorporated in 1915, it was practically a foregone conclusion that he would become mayor.

As were so many other things in South Florida, the growth of the city was set off by Henry Flagler's Florida East Coast Railway. A spur

Raulerson's general store, in use from 1905 to 1915.
(The Palm Beach Post)

line branching from the main tracks at New Smyrna Beach reached the area in the incorporation year, providing for the first time sure and fast contact with the outside world. Not only did the rails give cattlemen a better outlet for their product, but they also added impetus to two other industries that had sprung up: harvesting the abundant catfish from the big lake and cutting pine timber from the prairies to the north. FEC engineers laid out a town north of the 1915 settlement, with wide streets and a grassy mall linking the Taylor Creek siding with the main rails about a mile west. The FEC is gone, supplanted by CSX train service, but the mall remains the focus of the city. Lewis saw the new era coming and relocated his store, which had been on Taylor Creek about 150 yards from the original home, into a building that still faces the mall.

The new town may have had a government, but law and order were quite another matter. The area had three industries that drew rough-and-ready work forces. When the cowboys, lumberjacks, and fishermen hit town on Saturday night—their pockets full of the week's pay and their throats dry—things could get quite spirited. The area along Taylor Creek where the fishing boats tied up was always rowdy, according to historian Lawrence Will. In his *Cracker History of Okeechobee,* he describes the following scene: "I'm telling you, son, the crick was where you could see some action in the catfish days. . . . At Mr. Bryant's Rough House you could drink and gamble, while Johnson's Daylight Hotel always housed some friendly ladies. At the crick the boatmen fought to be first in line for ice, what time they weren't fighting for the pure pleasure of it."

One of the worst offenders was William E. "Pogey Bill" Collins, who had brawled his way from Australia to Chile to Tampa before taking up catfishing in 1910. When Justice of the Peace H. H. Hancock announced he was going to crack down on the outbursts at the Rough House, Pogey Bill's response was typical: he threatened to throw Hancock in the lake. He didn't get the chance. A group of men deputized by Hancock grabbed Collins and put him in one of the boxcars that served as a jail. After a trial punctuated by a few snide remarks from the defendant, Pogey Bill got ninety days in jail.

Carrying out the sentence on a man as popular with the brawlers as Pogey Bill became difficult, so, after a while, Hancock offered Collins a deal: commutation in return for his services on the right side of the law. Surprisingly, Pogey Bill agreed. First as city marshal and later as sheriff of Okeechobee County after it was created in 1917, Pogey Bill brought the brawling era to an end. His popularity was unparalleled until he ran afoul of federal law by looking the other way regarding moonshining. He was convicted in federal court in 1931 and resigned his office.

As the city of Okeechobee grew, the Raulerson family stayed in the center of civic affairs. Though, after the early years, Peter concentrated on his cattle business, other family members were active in the public sphere. Grandson John was on the County Commission that in 1926 built the present courthouse. Grandson Hiram spent twelve years as mayor and was in his twentieth year on the County Commission when he died in 1980. A grandnephew, O. L. Raulerson, was sheriff of Okeechobee County from 1986 until 1996.

As the decades went by, Peter Raulerson got older without seeming to. He still had a full head of curly hair, though it was snowy white, and his skin had few wrinkles. Into his ninth decade, Peter remained as lean as he always had been. And as popular. "He liked everybody," his daughter recalled. "He was very gregarious, almost to a fault." Though it no longer was courthouse-schoolhouse-post office, the Raulerson home continued to be a popular meeting place throughout Peter's life.

He was still riding to his herds at age eighty-eight, but he was fighting a losing battle to keep his stock free of screwworm. When the herd was disposed of, something seemed to leave Peter. He gradually became weaker, until he died on October 9, 1947, thirty-nine days after his ninetieth birthday.

The screwworm problem soon was solved, and the dairy industry embarked on a boom that peaked with fifty farms a decade ago. Since then, half the farms have been phased out because of Lake Okeechobee pollution. Meanwhile, the arc of vacation-weekend-retirement homes along the north shore of the big lake steadily expands. It may be just a matter of years before the industry that Peter Raulerson loved is history.

Sources for this chapter include *Lake Okeechobee* by Alfred Jackson Hanna and Kathryn Abbey Hanna; *A Cracker History of Okeechobee* by Lawrence E. Will; and interviews with Faith Raulerson Meserve and Hiram Raulerson.

Chapter 15
Tom Tiger
A Borrowed Horse and Stolen Bones

Without setting out to do so, Tom Tiger focused the nation's attention on the plight of Florida's Seminoles a century ago. In life, he was the catalyst for the first non-Indian group dedicated to helping the tribe. In death, he set off the nearest thing Florida has had to a twentieth-century uprising.

Tiger's prominence came somewhat from being in the right place at the right time: specifically, he was in South Florida when encroaching white settlement made the nation aware that Indians still lived on the peninsula, and that three wars and constant pressure from settlers had not eradicated the last of those bands who had slipped into Spanish Florida during the eighteenth century and had formed the Seminoles. Nevertheless, he also had qualities that fitted him for the role.

First, Tiger was an imposing person. Frederick A. Ober, one of the first whites to spend any time with the Florida Seminoles after the Third Seminole War, said in 1875, "He was over six feet in height, large and muscular. His eyes were black and fierce; his mouth—firm, but not cruel—was shaded by a small black mustache. We soon made friends with him and found him gentle and pleasant-voiced." Obviously, he was a natural hero for those in search of a Rousseauean noble savage. Second, he appears to have been one of the most influential members of the Cow Creek band, made up of Florida Seminoles who spoke a Muskogean language and lived on the savanna north of Lake Okeechobee, as opposed to the Mikasuki speakers who dwelt in the Everglades and in the Big Cypress Swamp of Southwest Florida.

Tiger—or Tustenuggee, to use his Indian name—undoubtedly was old enough to remember the Third Seminole War of 1858, though his exact age is unknown. In any case, he was old enough to command a following by the time the Seminoles had emerged from the two decades of isolation after the war, a period during which white America pretended all Seminoles had been either killed or shipped to Oklahoma. Those two hundred or so Indians who actually did remain stayed out of the settlers' way.

Cow Creek camps formed a rough arc from Fisheating Creek, on the west shore of Lake Okeechobee, northward around the lake, and south to the Indiantown area on the east. Some bands also had camps up the Kissimmee River. Their hunting range stretched from the lake north to the Blue Cypress Swamp and the headwaters of the St. Johns River, northwest into the higher timber country of the "Ridge" district, and east and south into Alligator Swamp, between Lake Okeechobee and the East Coast.

In the 1890s, most trading took place at Joe Bowers' camp at Indiantown; the stores run by Ben Hill Doster and Frank Bowers (Joe's brother) in Jupiter; Walter Kitching's store in Stuart; the Fort Pierce store run first by Benjamin Hogg and later by Peter P. Cobb; and the trading post at Basinger on the Kissimmee River, set up by Henry L. Parker. On occasion, however, the Cow Creeks would travel as far as Miami or Fort Lauderdale to trade. Noah Wilson, who came to the Palm Beaches in 1911, remembered Seminoles, presumably Mikasuki speakers, encamped on the ridge in West Palm Beach (in the area that today houses the federal building). In later years, bands would join townsmen for the Seminole Sun Dance celebration.

The incident that would first make Tiger famous outside his following occurred during the Christmas season in 1897. According to Tiger, Harmon H. Hull took a horse from Tiger's camp near Fort Drum, north of Lake Okeechobee, promising to return it in two months and pledging to do so in a statement written on a cartridge box. After several months had passed, Tiger demanded either the return of the horse or restitution; Hull denied having taken the animal. The proof, the cartridge-box document, had been obliterated during a rainstorm.

In the past, such an incident would have ended there. Because Indians were not citizens, they could not bring suit in state courts. Even if they could have, their chances of being believed would have been nil. But Tiger was not just any Indian. He was powerful and respected and had many friends, both Indian and non-Indian. In June of 1898, Tiger called on two of those non-Indian friends, James Willson and his wife, Minnie Moore-Willson, of Kissimmee. Two years earlier, Mrs. Willson had published *The Seminoles of Florida*, the first book written about the band since the Second Seminole

War. The Willsons, and others of like mind, realized that the Seminoles needed an organization to protect their rights and to acquire land on which they could lead their lives free of white interference. In January of 1899, they formed Friends of the Florida Seminoles, the group that provided the organizational and financial base needed to press Tiger's case.

On the basis of a complaint filed by Willson and attorney R. H. Seymour, Hull was charged with obtaining goods under false pretenses. Hull came to trial on April 28, 1899, in Titusville (Brevard County then stretched south to encompass all the land northeast of Lake Okeechobee). Though technically no Indians were parties to the case, Tiger and Billy Ham, another Cow Creek Seminole, did testify under oath, setting a precedent for Florida courts.

Tom Tiger.
(Seminole/Miccosukee Photographic Archive)

Mrs. Willson, who never was known to shy away from flowery adjectives, described Tiger's turn on the witness stand: "Captain Tom Tiger [it is unclear why Tiger frequently was given the title captain] was the first Florida Indian that ever stood up in a white man's court, making, as the spectators remarked, the most imposing picture they had ever witnessed. The tall, magnificent-looking savage, with uplifted hand, took the oath on the Holy Book, with a perfect understanding of its meaning. . . . The Indian never swerved under the strongest cross-examination, but told the story simply and direct."

Nevertheless, Tiger would not prevail. Because neither of the Indians could read, they could not swear that they knew, firsthand, what the cartridge-box statement had said. After the presentation of all evidence, Judge M. S. Jones announced that "there was no case against Hull and instructed the jury to bring in a verdict of acquittal," Mrs. Willson wrote. There apparently was much sympathy for the Indians, though, because court officials were among those who contributed money to buy Tiger another horse. More importantly, the incident gave Friends of the Florida Seminoles statewide publicity that drew attention to the Indians' plight and adherents to their cause.

Tiger returned to life as before, trapping and raising hogs at his camp in the Bluefield district, north of Lake Okeechobee. His day in court probably would have been the most famous incident concerning him if it hadn't been for his bizarre death and its equally bizarre aftermath. Shortly after the turn of the century, he was working on a dugout canoe when a storm blew up and a lightning bolt struck and killed him. When his family found his body, they turned the half-finished canoe over to create a burial vault rather than build the traditional Seminole log-pen grave.

In January of 1907, John T. Flournoy visited the frontier town of Tantie (now Okeechobee), saying he had come to write a history of the Indians. He collected as much data and as many artifacts as he could. Among them were Tom Tiger's bones and pipe, which he had obtained after a white trader named Barber had led him to the isolated grave site. According to an account in the *St. Lucie County Tribune*, "Mr. Flournoy told his companions that he intended to place the skeleton of Tom Tiger in the Smithsonian Institute [sic], and after returning to Tantie, brought them to Fort Pierce in a box and shipped them north. Mr. Flournoy left on the same train."

On February 23, Cow Creek medicine man Billie Smith came to Tantie and announced to Peter Raulerson, a good friend of the Indians, "Indians will go to war unless bones brought back in one moon [month]." When Raulerson asked how much money it would take to settle the matter, Smith was adamant: "No want money, want bones of best friend brought back; not bring back, Indians all fight, kill white man ojus [plenty]." Whether the Indians, few in number and beaten in three wars, would have attacked if nothing had been done is hard to say, but the threat certainly had an effect, both in Tantie and in Fort Pierce. Raulerson packed up his wife and younger children and sent them to Basinger. People in Fort Pierce were nervous enough to shoot at anything that moved in the night; one hardware store even played on the emotions, stressing that it had plenty of weapons and ammunition in stock.

The unease persisted throughout the spring, as James Willson pursued the matter by writing to the Smithsonian. The institution answered his letter in April, disclaiming any role in the removal of the bones and identifying Flournoy as the general manager of an amusement park in Johnstown, Pennsylvania. The letter said Flournoy had written to try to sell the skeleton, but that the institution would have nothing to do with the matter, now that it knew the artifacts had been obtained fraudulently. The Smithsonian also forwarded Willson's letter to Flournoy, who replied, denying any wrongdoing but saying he would be in Florida in June.

By the time Flournoy showed up, the hysteria had run its course, motivating the Pennsylvanian to bring the bones with him. The skeleton was returned to its resting place, and life in the area returned to normal. Flournoy apparently never was prosecuted. As Harry A. Kersey Jr. notes in a *Florida Historical Quarterly* article, the white reaction to the threat of violence showed how close to the surface the fear of an Indian massacre lurked. But it also rekindled interest in the Indians and concern that white incursions not destroy their lifestyle and culture.

Nevertheless, help was slow in coming. The only land the Friends of the Florida Seminoles was able to buy was lost because of taxes. Three reservations occupied today by members of the Seminoles Tribe of Florida were set aside in 1911 but not developed until some time later. Today, most Cow Creek Seminoles live on the Brighton Reservation northwest of Lake Okeechobee, while Mikasuki speakers occupy the reservations at Hollywood and Big Cypress. The separately incorporated Miccosukee Tribe of Florida has headquarters on the Tamiami Trail. Historically, the Cow Creeks have specialized in cattle, though in recent years, they have branched out into bingo, as have the Mikasuki speakers.

Roughly two thousand Seminoles live on the various reservations, though many Indians do not and thus are little noticed among the general population. The 1995 *Florida Statistical Abstract* lists 1,211 Native Americans (including Eskimos and Aleuts) in Palm Beach County, 543 in Hendry County, 431 in Glades County, 347 in St. Lucie County, 179 in Martin County, 145 in Okeechobee County, and 136 in Indian River County. Of these, only Glades County has a reservation.

As for Tom Tiger, his bones presumably rest, to this day, in a wilderness location perhaps not known to any living person.

Primary sources for this chapter include *The Seminoles of Florida* by Minnie Moore-Willson; "The Case of Tom Tiger's Horse: An Early Foray into Indian Rights" by Harry A. Kersey Jr.; and an anonymous article in the *St. Lucie County Tribune*.

Chapter 16

Bolles and Bryant
Drawing for a Farm

Sandwiched between the Flagler boom of the 1890s and the Roaring Twenties was a lesser known but just as spectacular period, set off by a populist governor's dream and buried amid the documents of congressional and grand-jury investigations. The goal was to turn the Everglades into one of the world's breadbaskets, but the effects weren't limited to this swampy environment. The city of Lake Worth was a by-product, and, more indirectly, the development fever led to the founding of Palm City and Port Salerno in Martin County and the first subdivision in Riviera Beach, as well as increased growth in other towns. In the Everglades, present-day settlements along the south shore of Lake Okeechobee, with the exception of Clewiston, got their start then. So did a number of other towns, such as Glades Crest and Okeelanta, that no longer exist.

Among the leaders of this time were one of the youngest persons ever to hold a seat on the New York Stock Exchange along with a Cambridge-trained agricultural pioneer. The former, Richard J. Bolles, was the best-known and most controversial figure of the period. At one time, he controlled five hundred thousand acres in Florida. In their book *Lake Okeechobee*, Alfred Jackson Hanna and Kathryn Abbey Hanna called him "the most spectacular, most ingenious and most criticized promoter of and speculator in Everglades land. . . . His ebullient humor and fund of anecdote were said to have made him a social favorite."

Bolles, a native of New York City, obtained his Big Board seat in 1866, at the age of twenty-three. He sold out in 1885 and joined the Colorado silver boom, only to enter real estate development as the boom faded about 1900. Through massive water-control systems, he turned hundreds of thousands of acres of near-desert into farms varying in size from ten to one thousand acres.

It was his irrigation project that brought him into contact with another man who would figure prominently in the future of southeast Florida. An Englishman thirty years Bolles' junior, F. Edward

Richard J. Bolles.
(The Bolles School)

F. Edward Bryant.
(Museum of the City of Lake Worth)

Bryant had come to the United States in 1894 to study agricultural methods and became particularly intrigued with water problems in the West. He evidently met Bolles in New Mexico when Bolles was considering a development there. The possibilities intrigued Bryant.

In 1908, a third figure entered the picture: Governor Napoleon Bonaparte Broward, an aggressive populist who had ridden to fame—and the governorship in 1904—by running guns to Cuban rebels. Broward believed the Florida Everglades could become one of the world's great agricultural areas, if only it could be drained. The Legislature went along, but powerful landowners tied up in court his efforts to float bonds to finance the drainage. Broward's only out was to raise the money by selling state land. But he needed a wealthy buyer, which is where Bolles came in. Broward went to Colorado and convinced the land baron to buy five hundred thousand acres at two dollars an acre. With Bolles' down payment in hand, the dredges were launched.

Others soon joined the rush, including the Everglades Land Sales Company and the Florida Everglades Land Company. Bryant, in partnership with his older brother, Harold, contracted for more than sixty thousand acres and formed the Palm Beach Farms Company; Bolles established the Florida Fruit Land Company. And both the Bryants and Bolles prepared to sell off their holdings in a novel, and soon to be controversial, manner. They subdivided their Everglades holdings into tracts of various sizes and laid out coastal town sites in lots twenty-five feet wide.

Bolles' town was called Progresso and was just north of the unincorporated village of Fort Lauderdale. The Bryants' was called Lucerne and was between West Palm Beach and Lantana, in an area that had been known as Jewell. Each farm was sold for the same price, and each purchaser received a free town lot. The location and size of each buyer's farm were determined in a drawing. The Progresso drawing of 1911 attracted so many people that a tent city was necessary, and on April 16, 1912, similar crowds came to West Palm Beach for the Lucerne drawing, which was handled by the company the Bryants formed with William Greenwood.

"As the date for drawing approached, many dreaming of lush lands and a promising future converged," according to Francis E. Love, whose father would be the first elected mayor of Lucerne. "Many, particularly those from the West and Midwest, came with their farming equipment, ready to start tilling their tracts. The first drawing was held in West Palm Beach at Okeechobee Road and South Dixie Highway with each buyer allowed to pull a slip from a box. Each slip held the legal description of the tract and the lot in Lucerne. For absentee owners, representatives were appointed to draw the slips."

The Love family drew a five-acre farm west of Delray Beach and a lot at what now is First Avenue South and M Street in Lake Worth. Immediately, there was a problem. "Just about this time Lucerne had a heavy rain, a cloudburst, and people went looking for their land in rowboats," Love said. Things soon picked up, however, and by December, the settlers were ready for both a post office and a charter. It was then they found out that Florida already had a Lucerne and that they needed a new name. The one they chose was Lake Worth, despite misgivings by some that the city and the lake would be confused in the minds of visitors.

Meanwhile, settlement was coming to the south end of Lake Okeechobee, an area that had been virtually unoccupied for two centuries even though it had been populated by Native Americans for about 2,500 years. According to historian Lawrence E. Will, the population of the south shore in 1910 consisted of four homesteaders, a few squatters, a hunter or two, and a dredge crew. The next year,

Bolles built the first new structure, a two-story hotel, at Ritta (now Lake Harbor) to house prospective purchasers. As the major drainage canals—Miami, North and South New River, Hillsboro, and Palm Beach—were dug, settlements grew on their shores and along the lake. Glades Crest on the Hillsboro Canal and Okeelanta on the North New River Canal were started in 1913, the latter by Will's father, Dr. Thomas E. Will.

As the level of the lake lowered, islands near the south shore appeared. The farmers who settled the largest of these, Torrey Island (opposite the Hillsboro Canal outlet), provided the beginning of what in 1928 would become Belle Glade. And the East Beach area began growing into what in 1917 would be incorporated as Pahokee. Other settlements included Canal Point on the Palm Beach Canal, South Bay on the North New River Canal, and Bare Beach a few miles west of South Bay.

Loading beans onto a boat at Pahokee, 1925.
(The Palm Beach Post)

The most extensive early development, however, was in the area where the Disston canal to the Caloosahatchee River leaves Lake Okeechobee. It was marked by a tall cypress tree that still stands. In 1915, James A. Moore, who made a fortune subdividing in Seattle and lost most of it trying to establish an ironworks in the Pacific Northwest, bought ninety-eight thousand acres southwest of the lake and laid out the town of Moore Haven. Though Moore, himself, would not last there, the settlement was soon incorporated and began to draw residents from outside the area and from nearby lake settlements. In 1921, Moore Haven became the seat of the new Glades County.

But development wasn't restricted to those areas directly affected by Everglades land sales. In 1910, Charles N. Newcomb, a wealthy industrialist and inventor of a loom, filed the first Palm Beach County plat in today's Riviera Beach (the same plat had been filed earlier in Dade County). Newcomb, who had filled in the lake shore with a dredge of his own design, did not achieve his dreams of building a major tourist center, but he did set off development in the small existing community, sparking what would become an incorporated community in 1922.

All this activity continued on a relatively even keel despite the fact that the original Everglades promotions had collapsed amid unrealized hopes and a series of investigations. To begin with, Broward's reasoning that canals would turn the Everglades into a breadbasket overnight was faulty. He did not realize that the Everglades was not a swamp but rather a "river of grass," as Marjory Stoneman Douglas put it in her 1947 book, or that water levels fluctuated with the seasons. The canals could not carry the water off quickly enough to prevent flooding in wet years or seasons, and they made the dry periods so dry that the rich, organic, muck soil sometimes burst into flames spontaneously. Beyond that, many of the tracts were inaccessible. The elder Will realized this and tried to talk major developers into exchanging such land for tracts near the canals, apparently with little success.

Also, the Everglades were not suitable for the small-scale farming many of the settlers had become accustomed to. Five- and ten-acre tracts were useless even if well-located. Much of the Everglades land sold by Bolles and by the Bryant and Greenwood firm never was occupied. Within a few years, the settlements of Okeelanta and Glades Crest were abandoned, and most of the settlers from Glades Crest moved to Moore Haven. "We had bought a tract that was west of Boynton and got a twenty-five-foot lot in town (Lake Worth)," pioneer Bertha Gainer recalled. "But we never saw the tract and let it go for taxes."

More serious for the developers, though, were the accusations that the properties had been misrepresented and that the drawings were illegal lotteries. Five people were convicted in a Missouri trial—many of the buyers were from Missouri—because of bad claims and sales methods. Bolles might have even been hauled into court had he not died on March 25, 1917, on a train between West Palm Beach and Jacksonville.

Meanwhile, Bryant had turned his attention again to agriculture rather than development. During the World War I sugar shortage, he became interested in the potential of an Everglades sugar industry and was instrumental in getting an Agriculture Department cane-breeding station established at Canal Point. He and his associates organized the Florida Sugar and Food Products Company, and in 1921 constructed the first sugar mill in the Everglades. He later presided over the growth of U.S. Sugar and was on the first city commission when Clewiston was incorporated in 1931.

At age seventy-two, he still was superintendent of U.S. Sugar's eastern division. He was on his way to a field inspection December 6, 1945, when his car got bogged down in the muck. While attempting to free it, he suffered a heart attack and died before he could be taken back to company headquarters.

Sources for this chapter include *Lake Okeechobee* by Alfred Jackson Hanna and Kathryn Abbey Hanna; *Florida from Indian Trail to Space Age* by Charlton Tebeau; *Florida: Historic, Dramatic, Contemporary* by J. E. Dovell; "Early Days of Lucerne—Now Lake Worth—Were Exciting, Pioneer Settler Recalls" by Steve Korpan; the files of the Lake Worth Public Library; and the following anonymous articles: "F. Edw. Bryant Dies at Azucar"; "Four Indicted in Everglades Inquiry"; "Richard J. Bolles Dies Suddenly on F.E.C. Train."; and "Richard J. Bolles—The Man Behind the Name."

Chapter 17

Marian Newhall Horwitz O'Brien
The Lady Was a Mayor

Marian Newhall Horwitz O'Brien was someone different in the agricultural frontier that was the south shore of Lake Okeechobee. Born into wealth in Philadelphia on August 13, 1880, she was an aristocrat in a milieu where women were judged more by the amount of manual labor they could perform than by their family trees. She was independent in a time when women were supposed to be submissive. And she was tolerant in a time and place where toleration extended only to white Protestants. She was a founding leader of two towns, Moore Haven and Clewiston; president of the railroad that connected them; and mayor of Moore Haven at a time when women still could not vote in Florida elections. Then violence pushed her out of the Everglades, though not before she had become known as the Duchess of Moore Haven.

Marian Newhall became Marian Newhall Horwitz in 1899, when she married attorney George Quintard Horwitz. Soon well known in both civic and social affairs, the couple had many friends, John J. O'Brien of the *Philadelphia Public Ledger* among them. O'Brien, acting as an agent for Atlantic City developer Clarence M. Busch, headed south to investigate talk that had filtered north about rich farmland near Lake Okeechobee. He found ninety-eight thousand good acres owned by James A. Moore, who had run into financial trouble in 1916 and was eager to sell. Busch bought Moore's land, and O'Brien and Horwitz wound up with thirty-six hundred acres, including the Moore Haven town site. Before the O'Brien-Horwitz firm could get going, however, Horwitz died.

Mrs. Horwitz visited Moore Haven for the first time in February of 1917 and liked what she saw. She became active in promoting the new community. She was well-equipped to do so. One contemporary described her as a woman who had everything: wealth, good looks, charm, and ability. According to *Lake Okeechobee*, a book by Alfred Jackson Hanna and Kathryn Abbey Hanna:

She knew everybody, had been everywhere, was accustomed to enjoying the best the world had to offer and, in the best Philadelphia tradition, she made a full accounting of her stewardship of wealth, position, time and ability to civic and philanthropic organizations.

Her figure was slender, her skin was fair, her hair flaxen and her eyes were of a greenish-hazel shade. With personal magnetism, courage and energy, she was abundantly endowed.

She threw herself wholeheartedly into the development of Moore Haven and the welfare of its people as she conceived these objectives. She and her partner, O'Brien, built and stocked a general store and organized a bank. She was head of both enterprises and also of a vegetable exchange, a development company and the DeSoto Stock Farms Company. She rose early and by daylight was out on her farms, which she operated with the most modern machinery available.

The Moore Haven to which Mrs. Horwitz had come was a man's town in more ways than one. A year before her arrival, there had been only three women in town, one of them a development company employee who moonlighted as a prostitute. Farm wives were expected to be both productive and submissive. The town, however, would break new ground. When it was organized late in 1917, its charter gave women the right to vote in city elections, even though they would not be able to vote in state elections until adoption of the Nineteenth Amendment to the Constitution in 1920. (In 1921, Moore Haven— until then in DeSoto County— would become seat of the new Glades County.)

Perhaps Moore Haven did not fear female voting power because it had so few women. In any case,

Marian Newhall Horwitz O'Brien.
(Glades County)

it obviously did not fear power in the hands of Mrs. Horwitz, for she was chosen charter mayor, one of the first female mayors in the nation. About the same time, she became Mrs. John J. O'Brien, at least in part so she could manage the couple's business affairs when John was called up for World War I duty with his Pennsylvania National Guard unit.

These were bright years for the young town. Weather conditions were good, and the rich soil was productive. In 1917 alone, the farmers shipped one hundred thousand bushels of potatoes down the Disston canal. The next year, the arrival of the Atlantic Coast Line railroad made shipping considerably easier. The O'Briens should have been on top of the world, but they weren't.

"Much as they did for Moore Haven and attractive as they were personally, [the O'Briens] bore certain handicaps for life in a rural, fundamentalist Southern community. They were Northern, wealthy and O'Brien was a Roman Catholic," the Hannas explained in their book. "Any one of these characteristics might have been overlooked; all together, they were overpowering. Little, absurd bits fed the flame. The O'Briens wore riding breeches and traveled on horseback much of the time, a common-sense practice, but more than a shade different from that of anyone else."

Marian O'Brien's nonconformities were mitigated by her graciousness, but her husband's were aggravated by his brusque manner and impatience. On top of that, Florida was in a period of anti-Catholic nativism marked by the imprisonment of three nuns in their St. Augustine convent and the dismissal of a Fort Lauderdale teacher because of her religion. To compound their problems, the O'Briens tried to found a town three miles northwest of Moore Haven primarily for Englishmen and bearing Mrs. O'Brien's maiden name, Newhall.

The community, the Hannas say, "marked a new idiosyncrasy. The newcomers, though educated and gentle, were foreigners of odd behavior; they drank tea each afternoon and the wives smoked cigarettes in long holders. Furthermore, their presence gave the O'Briens the status of lord and lady of the manor. That the venture lost out all the way around was no counter-irritant."

All of this may have been forgiven if the O'Briens hadn't committed the ultimate sin of bringing in African-American field hands. African-Americans had been imported to work on the railroad, but that was temporary, whereas the field hands would be permanent residents. Some of the other settlers made it clear they did not want African-American neighbors. " 'Cow hunters' hid in the brush along the [railroad] right-of-way and took pot shots at the Negroes as they worked on many farms," the Hannas wrote. "White labor walked out as soon as the Negroes walked in. Mayor O'Brien was equal to the crisis. Farmers and businessmen were organized into vigilance committees, some of the more violent hoodlums were jailed, and after two days the war was over. The Negroes continued to work. It was a victory for her honor the mayor, but not one which endeared her to certain segments of the population."

In 1920, undeterred by the failure of the town of Newhall, the O'Briens decided to branch out again, this time to the southeast. Their target was known then as Sand Point, populated only by a small colony of Japanese. "The O'Briens, with the backing of Alonzo C. Clewis, president of the Exchange National Bank at Tampa, bought a tract of land. Then for $10,000 they hired John Nolan, a prominent city planner, to lay out a city [that they named for Clewis]," Lawrence E. Will wrote in *Cracker History of Okeechobee*. "Their next move after that was to start building a railroad, the Moore Haven and Clewiston."

Besides a depot, the O'Briens built docks on the end of the point. Inland, Nolan laid out the wide streets and open space that characterize Clewiston to this day. "The O'Briens built a comfortable home on the ridge about a mile from depot and docks," according to a special edition of the *Clewiston News*, published in 1973 for the golden anniversary of Hendry County. (Hendry County had been cut from Lee County and named for Francis Asbury Hendry, a leading figure in southwest Florida for fifty years following the Civil War). "Near the center of activity they built a two-story frame building which housed a general store and restaurant on the first floor and had 20 hotel rooms above. They placed a Japanese couple in charge and gave the hotel their name, the Watanabe." Once again, the O'Briens organized a bank. And their home was open to visiting dignitaries, notably Thomas Alva Edison.

Their good fortune soon would end. For one thing, the weather honeymoon was over. Unknown to the residents, the years 1916 to 1921 had been unusually dry. Though this had led to muck fires, it also, for the most part, had led to good crops. In 1922, the rains came, and it soon became evident that the drainage system only worked when there wasn't much water. The small sugar mill that had been built at Moore Haven the previous year went out of business. And among the crops lost were seven hundred acres of tomatoes, particularly unfortunate because the price was high that year. "Vegetables, even if they had matured, couldn't be hauled from the fields with tractors and wagons, not even with sleds," Will wrote. The flooding also wiped out the avocado industry at Ritta (now Lake Harbor).

The O'Briens were running into the same hatred in Clewiston that they had had to overcome in Moore Haven. This time, they would not prevail. O'Brien insisted in later years that the trouble stemmed from his religion, but that seems to have been only one factor. Another was—as was the case in Moore Haven—African-American field hands. On top of that, his hurried ways irritated the residents, who preferred a slower pace. O'Brien arranged for a Catholic priest to come from Tampa every six weeks to say Mass in his house. Most of those in attendance were Frenchmen and Belgians who had come to the area to found Lakeport, on the west side of Lake Okeechobee.

"One night a shot was fired into the O'Brien home," the Hannas wrote, "and, although probably intended for O'Brien, it hit Mrs. O'Brien and made an ugly wound on her scalp. . . . She dashed out into the jungle armed with a revolver but, in the darkness, she was unable to find her assailant. A crisis was reached when the O'Brien house was burned and from it were rescued only a small pup and a blue bowl. Mrs. O'Brien remained in a hotel room until some friends sewed clothes sufficient for an escape to quieter surroundings in Palm Beach."

She would never return to the Everglades. The O'Briens spent the rest of the Roaring Twenties in Palm Beach, later living in Philadelphia, then Detroit. In 1932, while O'Brien was on an anti-Prohibition speaking tour, his wife contracted pneumonia and lapsed into a coma. He rushed back to their Grosse Point home, but she never regained consciousness. She died on May 8 at age fifty-one.

A word that is consistent throughout the many descriptions of Marian Newhall Horwitz O'Brien is "vivid." The anti-Prohibition organization for which both of the O'Briens had worked eulogized her by saying she had "a vivid personality, a spirit of charity." Her only child, Dr. Orville Horwitz of Philadelphia, said, "She had the most vivid, really sparkling personality of anyone I have ever known.

She was extremely attractive, extremely warm and generous." She was also a driving force in the birth of two cities, quite a testament in itself.

Sources for this chapter include *Lake Okeechobee* by Alfred Jackson Hanna and Kathryn Abbey Hanna; *A Cracker History of Okeechobee* by Lawrence E. Will; a telephone interview with Dr. Orville Horwitz; and an anonymous article in the *Clewiston News*.

Chapter 18

Harry Seymour Kelsey
Boom and Bust

Harry Seymour Kelsey knew how to spot a trend. First, there was the fast-lunch business. He got into it almost by accident but nevertheless developed the concept into a chain of 112 restaurants, bakeries, and commissaries. Then, there was the twenties Florida land boom. He began buying land in 1919, and his Kelsey City (today's Lake Park) is believed to have been the first zoned community in Florida. But, finally, there was the bust. If Kelsey's 1925 sale of most of his property had not fallen through, he would have been largely out from under his debt before the collapse in land values of early 1926—plus the hurricanes of that year and 1928—retarded Florida's development until World War II.

As if bust and blow weren't enough, Kelsey also had problems with the Internal Revenue Service. The government took the $1.6 million he had received from the sale of today's Intracoastal Waterway and applied it to back taxes, and Kelsey was for six years under a federal indictment that included criminal charges. Even so, he fared better than many of the boom-time developers. Although he had lost millions, he managed to somewhat rebuild his fortunes through such ventures as patent dealing and a pharmaceutical firm. He was looking to get back into Florida real estate, with a development west of Miami named Utopia, when he died in 1957.

Kelsey was born on March 26, 1879, in Claremont, New Hampshire, and grew up on a farm outside Springfield, Massachusetts. He became a successful stockbroker in Springfield but, interestingly enough, it was an unsuccessful trade that led him into the restaurant business. Specifically, he found himself with a large stock of unsellable restaurant equipment. Making the best of a bad deal, he leased a storefront and opened a quick-lunch restaurant, a novelty in those times. He ended up building a chain of restaurants that he would sell for three million dollars.

His interest in Florida development began in the opening days of 1919, when he visited Palm Beach to rest up after a bout of pneumonia and to see the building lot a friend had bought for him at auction.

He arrived on New Year's Day and, two days later, his friend introduced him to a broker named Harry Greene. Evidently, Greene didn't have to do much persuading. According to Kelsey himself, "That morning I bought forty-four thousand acres of land about ten miles west of [the ocean] known as the Old Barr Estate."

During the next two years, Kelsey heavily invested his restaurant proceeds into Florida land. Among his holdings were the future sites of North Palm Beach and Lake Park and the older section of Palm Beach Gardens, as well as fourteen miles of oceanfront between Miami and Jupiter, including the oceanfront section of North Palm Beach and the Seminole Golf Club property.

The prosperity set off by the end of World War I was manifesting itself in many ways, and one of those was the rush to Florida. A new era had dawned, and the bad experiences of those caught up in the drainage land boom a decade earlier had been forgotten. Kelsey hired the Boston planning firm of Olmstead Brothers, designers of Central Park in New York City, to lay out his town. Tourist courts—the forerunners of today's motels—and trailers were banned, and areas were allocated for homes, recreation, business, and industry. It was to be a city for those who worked. "Kelsey City had everything,"

Harry Seymour Kelsey.
(The Palm Beach Post)

recalled Bryan Poston, who was born there in 1925. "There was a ballroom, brick factory, an icehouse and ice-cream plant, automobile showrooms on Park Avenue, a lumberyard cutting two hundred thousand feet of pine and cypress a day, banks, theaters, restaurants, playgrounds and parks."

As the boom progressed, relatively stable developers like Kelsey were joined by others who seemed to have no visible assets other than dreams and adjectives. Picture City, a planned community near Hobe Sound that was to include a one million dollar motion picture studio, never amounted to much more than a water tank. Today it is marked by nothing except pairs of aging concrete lampposts along the west side of State Road A1A, north of Bridge Road. Nearby Olympia did little more than provide a name for the community until it eventually was changed to Hobe Sound. The central hub of Olympia, which was laid out to resemble an Olympic arena, is now the Hobe Sound ball field complex.

And then there was Indrio, in north St. Lucie County. A series of ads in *Time* magazine showed renderings of "proposed" plazas, bathing casinos, and railway stations and "suggested treatments" of homes in the adapted Mediterranean style of Coral Gables. This version of "America's Most Beautiful Home Town" never got beyond that stage.

As Kelsey City blossomed, other cities filled in areas that had been little more than laid out during previous development. Towns were being reincorporated as cities. Older unincorporated settlements were obtaining charters, so they either could have the services provided in the new communities or avert annexation by them. And others were virtually springing from the ground. As the 1920s began, the area had only ten incorporated municipalities, the oldest of which was West Palm Beach (1894). Others were Fort Pierce (1901), Delray Beach and Palm Beach (1911), Lake Worth (1913), Stuart (1914), Okeechobee (1915), Pahokee and Moore Haven (1917), and Vero Beach (1919). Boynton Beach got its charter in 1920, followed by Lantana in 1921, Riviera Beach in 1922, and Kelsey City in 1923. Boca Raton and Jupiter came into corporate being in 1925, Greenacres and Gulf Stream in 1926, Sewall's Point in 1927, and Belle Glade in 1928.

W. J. "Fingy" Connors, who had made a fortune bossing stevedores on the Buffalo docks, bought everything available between Canal Point and Okeechobee—about twelve thousand acres—and linked his holdings to the coast with a toll road from Twenty-Mile Bend to Okeechobee roughly on the right-of-way of today's U.S. 98. It would have been the first link between the coast and Lake Okeechobee had the road that today is Old State Road 80 not been completed just months earlier. Fort Pierce Inlet was dug in 1921 to replace the old Indian River Inlet, which had silted closed for the final time in 1910.

Stories of tremendous profits were legion and further fueled the mania. A Palm Beach tract that sold for eight hundred thousand dollars in 1923 supposedly was worth four million dollars just two years

Clematis Street, West Palm Beach, in the 1920s.
(The Palm Beach Post)

later. A poor woman who had bought land near Miami in 1896 for twenty-five dollars sold it in 1925 for $150,000. Paris Eugene Singer, the sewing-machine heir, paid $1.75 million in 1925 for 250 lakefront acres adjacent to Kelsey City that had gone for a few hundred dollars several years earlier.

In November of 1925, Kelsey branched out. He bought the Florida East Coast Canal, an inland waterway that had been dug from Jacksonville to Miami late in the nineteenth century but had never fulfilled its promise due to dredging and silting problems. He planned to improve it so it could handle freight barges. The need was clear: native stands of lumber had been exhausted, and the technology for mass-producing concrete blocks had not yet been developed, which meant that building materials had to be shipped in either by sea or on the single-track Florida East Coast Railway. Even the two combined were inadequate. During the summer of 1925, the FEC, expecting the usual hot-weather slump, cut back on operations to double-track its system.

Instead, the boom kept booming, and building materials piled up at Jacksonville. By the time the FEC realized what had happened, it was too late to make headway against the ever-growing backlog. On October 29, an embargo was declared south of Jacksonville on everything except food or items for which special permits had been obtained. The effect was quick and dramatic. A lot in West Palm Beach that was supposed to be the site of "one of the most magnificent apartment buildings in the South," for instance, instead became the graveyard of hundreds of crated bathtubs, the only item to arrive before the embargo.

The nature of the South Florida boom exacerbated the problem. Speculation had been so frantic that buyers were taking on huge obligations, confident they would be able to sell before the bills came due. For this to work, more and more money had to flow into the state. In February of 1926, Trust Company of Florida was offering eight percent compound interest, about two percent above the prevailing rate, to attract more money.

The effort was futile. By this time, Northern banks had gotten nervous and had started to tighten up on credit. The momentum continued downward, and the house of cards began to collapse. Buyers began defaulting en masse, including the Dallas businessmen who had agreed in 1925 to buy Kelsey's undeveloped mainland holdings for $30 million. As Frederick Lewis Allen put it in his book *Only Yesterday*, "There were cases in which the land came back to the original owner, but came back burdened with taxes and assessments which amounted to more than the cash he had received for it; and furthermore he found his land blighted with a half-completed development."

Some felt the collapse would be a long-range blessing because it would weed out the fly-by-nights and allow firms such as Kelsey's to resume growth at a saner level. They had not counted on the Big Wind. Just as Kelsey was building a laundry for his city, the great hurricane of September 17–18, 1926, roared northwest from Miami to Lake Okeechobee, splintering developments as far north as Pompano Beach and killing 300–400 people when Lake Okeechobee's dike burst at Moore Haven. There was little damage in Palm Beach County, but bleak headlines in Northern newspapers scared off buyers.

Besides, Kelsey had problems all his own. According to Charles Branch, who was general manager of Kelsey's East Coast Financial Corporation, they stemmed from Kelsey's dislike for day-to-day business operations. He turned most of the detail work over to others.

Branch says that when Kelsey came on board in 1925, an associate asked him, "When are you going to start stealing from the old man? Everyone else is." More seriously, says Branch, Kelsey signed his tax returns without ever reading them. And, according to the Internal Revenue Service, those returns seriously understated his income.

When Kelsey sold the canal to the state in 1927, his proceeds were seized and applied to back taxes. And when the government found out that his cost for acquiring an oceanfront tract had been overstated by a factor of ten, more dramatic action was taken. Not only were liens of eight hundred thousand dollars against East Coast and two hundred thousand dollars against Kelsey filed, but Kelsey also was indicted on criminal charges. Once again, Kelsey survived. He stayed in business and eventually won dismissal of the indictment on the basis that the error was the inadvertent misplacement of a decimal point.

Then came the hurricane of September 16, 1928, straight over the Palm Beaches. Damage to Kelsey City was estimated at one million dollars in material terms; in terms of image, it was incalculable. Kelsey tried to rebuild, but there was no more money, "and I had to let the whole thing go." The buyer was Sir Harry Oakes, who was a New England native like Kelsey but flamboyant in contrast to the reserved Kelsey. Oakes spent a lot on his Florida holdings before he was murdered in Nassau in 1943, but there was little to show for it due to the Depression. In 1939, Kelsey City was renamed Lake Park.

As for Kelsey, he returned to New England and busied himself in patent trading and pharmaceuticals. He dabbled in other Florida developments with little success but rarely returned to the city he had founded except for a visit at the city's request in 1950. He died in Orlando on November 27, 1957.

Biographical information for this chapter comes largely from "Biographies of Prominent Men: Harry Seymour Kelsey" (anonymous article). Other sources include "Early Days of Lucerne—Now Lake Worth—Were Exciting, Pioneer Settler Recalls" by Steve Korpan; "The Intracoastal: Rich in History and Natural Beauty" by Ann Carter; "Former Boston Man Sees the Florida City He Started in 1922 'Come to Life'" by W. E. L. Lush; various anonymous articles in *The Palm Beach Post* and *The Palm Beach Times*; and an interview with Charles Branch.

Chapter 19
Addison Cairns Mizner
The Architect as an Artist

Where do you start telling the story of Addison Mizner? Do you pick Palm Beach, where he turned a somewhat frumpy and swampy playground into an American Riviera? How about Boca Raton, where he dreamed impossible dreams and made a few of them come true? What of Guatemala, where he first was drawn to Mediterranean architecture? Or Spain, where he honed his skills? Then there's the Klondike, where he mined gold; Australia, where he earned his way out by prizefighting; Honolulu, where he was decorated by an ex-queen; Shanghai, where he sold casket handles.

Addison Cairns Mizner.
(The Palm Beach Post)

Mizner was a giant of a man, six-foot-three and 275 pounds, with a sense of humor to match. He didn't mind making himself the butt of a joke. If you want to start off with a good anecdote, just flip to any page of his autobiography.

When Mizner came to Palm Beach in 1918, the social center was the Royal Poinciana Hotel, a rambling wooden structure that even Henry Flagler's friends conceded was not one of his better efforts. When Mizner died about fifteen years later, the focus had shifted south to Mizner's Everglades Club, and the pillars of society lived in his villas. He was not the only noted architect to focus on Palm Beach during the Roaring Twenties—others include Marion Sims Wyeth, Maurice Fatio, Howard Major, John L. Volk, and Joseph Urban (designer of Mar-a-Lago)—but he was the most flamboyant.

Few of his grandiose dreams for Boca Raton came true; most were cut off by the 1926 collapse of the Florida land boom. But among those that were realized are the magnificent older section of the Boca Raton Hotel and Club, the Floresta subdivision, and the expansive eastern leg of Camino Real.

As an architect, Mizner was unconventional and, therefore, controversial. He never finished his degree work at Salamanca in Spain, and the only examination he ever took for an architect's license was an unorthodox one in which he informally told of his work. He approached his trade more as an artist than as an engineer. But then, so did Michelangelo. Mizner's blueprints could be haphazard; sometimes he didn't even draw a set. Once, he sketched out a villa in the sand with a stick. He was a visionary and looked to others for engineering details.

The best that can be said for his style, which defied categorization, is that it is Spanish-inspired. Often, he would mix several periods in the same building, though not in the same room. Yet, in one important way, his buildings were unlike those of Spain. Mizner believed in ventilation and eschewed the solid outer walls of Iberia in favor of large windows. As he once explained, "A Spanish home is like a fort on the outside. . . . I turned the Spanish home inside out."

To furnish his buildings, he scoured Latin America and Europe for antiques. "I have looted cathedrals, churches and palaces," he once said, "and brought a shipload or two of everything from stone doorways to fine laces from both Central America and Europe." If there weren't enough old furnishings to go around, he would make his own. He started his own factories in West Palm Beach for furniture, stonework, stained glass, and tile. And he had his ways of making the new look old. One day, as Alva Johnston relates in *The Legendary Mizners*, he startled a workman by strolling into a room of a Palm Beach mansion nearing completion and using a hammer to whack off the nose and upturned toes of a grotesque stone dwarf by the fireplace. "You see," he said, "this house is supposed to be four or five centuries old. Hundreds of cords of wood have theoretically been carried into this room and dropped by this fireplace. Now, it's perfectly obvious that that long nose and those curled shoe tips must have been broken off long ago."

He would have his men apply acid, broken bottles, ice picks, chains, steel wool, and air rifles to architectural elements to simulate age. Roof tiles were broken deliberately and were set in place as irregularly as possible. When one roof looked too neat for him, he ordered down the men who were at work and sent up two who had never laid a tile in their lives.

Mizner had the manners of a gentleman when it suited him. He also could be earthy, as befits one who had been a miner and a prizefighter. He once lost a commission for telling an indecisive woman in the crudest terms possible to make up her mind. He was banished from the very Everglades Club he had built.

Addison Cairns Mizner was born on December 12, 1872, in Benicia, California, the seventh of eight children of Lansing Bond Mizner and Ella Watson Mizner. As a child, he could have been called the biggest hellion in Benicia had it not been for competition from older brothers William and Edgar and younger brother Wilson. More important were his teenage years. After a serious leg injury in 1888 laid him up for a year, he took up watercolors and became interested in art. The next year, his father was appointed United States envoy to the five Central American republics—Costa Rica, Nicaragua, Honduras, El Salvador, and Guatemala—and young Addison was introduced to Iberian architecture.

After studies in California and Spain, Mizner went into business as an architect in San Francisco, making a lot of drawings and very little money. Brother Edgar had a better idea. He had heard of a big gold strike on Bonanza Creek in the Yukon and talked brothers William, Addison, and Wilson into going north with him in 1897. By the time they had arrived, the news was out, and thousands of others also were on hand. After a year during which he escaped a plot by three hired hands to murder him and lost much of his gold to a crooked government inspector, Addison returned to San Francisco.

During the next few years, he wandered the Pacific. He was decorated by ex-Queen Liliuokalani of Hawaii for rescuing her medals from an attic of the royal palace in Honolulu, where they had lain unnoticed after she was expelled when the monarchy was overthrown. He painted magic-lantern slides in Samoa, won two thousand dollars boxing in Australia, and eventually paid for his way back home by selling casket handles.

While in Hawaii, he and author Ethel Watts Mumford published a Cynic's Calendar, which not only made him some money but also made certain circles aware of his work. In New York, aided by the

How to Wind a Road

Of all the tales about Addison Mizner, none is more flamboyant than the story of how the road was moved away from the ocean in Ocean Ridge. When Mizner bought up much of that area in the 1920s, the road ran along the ocean. As with many other things, he had his own ideas about this. One day, he met with his engineers at the site, with a stack of laths in his hand, and announced he was going to lay out a new road. "This is one time the architect precedes the engineer," he said. "Every place I put a lath, I want a bend in the road." Then he set off through the palmetto scrub, laying out the winding path that State Road A1A follows to this day between Boynton Inlet and Ocean Avenue.

The city of Boynton, which then included what today are Ocean Ridge and Briny Breezes, approved the relocation, but a local weekly newspaper mounted a campaign to have the work held up. Addison became impatient with the delays, said Karl Riddle, one of his engineers. "You get all the equipment you can find," he told Riddle, "and go down there and tear up the road." Riddle complied, and one evening shortly after dark, the work began. Before dawn, quite a few great stories—some true, some not—would be born.

The most spectacular, as recounted in Alva Johnston's *The Fabulous Mizners*, tells of Mizner's rogue brother Wilson standing in the light of construction flares, cursing loudly at a group of Finns who were trying to prevent their ocean access from being cut off. It's a great story, but Riddle says it just isn't so. It's true that Wilson did come by that night with some friends after a party and that all were formally dressed, Riddle said, but there was no confrontation. That would come later, about two o'clock in the morning, when sheriff's deputies descended to shut down the work and "arrested everyone in sight." Fortunately for Riddle, he wasn't in sight. At the first sound of the deputies, he had gone back to where the men had left their cars to dispense with the liquor they had brought for a post-construction party, since this was during Prohibition.

The road hassle was finally straightened out, and Mizner got his way. He already had begun to lose interest in the Boynton area, however, and never did carry through on any other development plans after that. Instead, he sold the land. Mizner today is memorialized in the area only by a road that winds as if it were laid out by an artist rather than an engineer. It was. ❖

publicity from the calendar, he became increasingly successful in both business and society. He completed some architectural work and sold some antiquities, but his was a peripatetic existence. In 1915, his mother, a lively woman to whom he had been devoted, died, and in 1917, a beating by hitchhikers reinjured his bad leg, forcing him to stay in bed for months.

This last turned out to be a blessing. First, the inactivity gave Addison time to think about his career. As Johnston put it: "When he had the use of his legs, he was perpetually busy with small things and neglected his creative talents. He had not been able to decide whether he was an artist, architect, interior decorator, landscape designer, curio peddler, fortune hunter, antiquarian, society ladies' pet, chow raiser, heiress chaser or literary man. His various professions and enthusiasms tended to destroy one another." Second, it turned him toward Florida. Joan Bates, an English nurse he met through sewing-machine heir Paris Eugene Singer, recommended a couple of months in Palm Beach to help heal his leg. The sunshine did the predicted wonders, and he soon was ready to help Singer realize his dream.

Singer, the youngest of twenty-four children of Isaac Merritt Singer, was a legend in his own right. "He was the finest-looking man I ever saw," Mizner said. "Six-feet-three or -four . . . with a fine figure. At this time [1917] he was fifty and looked forty. Of course he never understood me and I doubt if I ever understood him. Paris was a strange silent man who . . . was hard to talk to unless you got him on his own subjects. At this time it was hospital work." Singer wanted to build a convalescent center for wounded World War I soldiers. The architect didn't know that, however, the day Singer took him "down by the lake, where Worth Avenue begins to turn into Lake Drive," and asked him what he envisioned on the outside of the curve.

"It's so beautiful that it ought to be something religious," Mizner told him, "a nunnery with a chapel built into the lake, with great cool cloisters and a court of oranges. A landing stage where a stern old abbess could barter with boatmen bringing their fruit and vegetables for sale. A great gate over there on the road, where the faithful could leave their offering and receive largess. It could be a mixture, built by a nun from Venice, added onto by one from Gerona, with a bit of New Spain of the tropics. What a spot!"

To Mizner, just about any change in Palm Beach would have been an improvement: "They had spoiled as much of its natural beauty as possible. Where great jungles had stood, now ragged sand lots stared you in the face. On the next block was a horrible-looking monstrosity called Gus' Bath. And on the front was painted in huge letters, 'Welcome to Our Ocean.'" Another nearby "feature" was Joe's Alligator Farm.

Alligator Joe at his "farm," Palm Beach.
(The Palm Beach Post)

Singer let Mizner in on his plans, and Mizner was soon drawing sketches for the Touchstone Club for Convalescent Soldiers. Before it was completed, however, the war had ended, and it became instead the Everglades Club. The club made Mizner the most sought-after architect in town, as well as a social lion. Soon to follow were a series of magnificent villas with names such as El Mirasol and Playa Riente. Historian James Knott credits the architect with being instrumental in turning Palm Beach from a hotel resort into a city of magnificent

The Everglades Club seen from the lake side.
(The Palm Beach Post)

mansions. Across the street from the Everglades Club, Mizner built an arcade of shops, cut apart by the narrow winding paths named Via Mizner and Via Parigi. Mizner's own home opened off the former, which holds the grave of his pet monkey, Johnny Brown.

By 1925, Mizner had even grander plans. He was going to turn the small farming village of Boca Raton into "a happy combination of Venice and Heaven, Florence and Toledo, with a little Greco-Roman glory and grandeur thrown in." There would be palatial homes, broad thoroughfares, exquisite golf courses. A hotel to end all hotels would be connected with the Florida East Coast Railway by the broadest boulevard of all, Camino Real, two hundred feet wide with a canal down the center populated by gondolas. On February 6, 1926, Mizner opened his Cloister Inn, comprising what today is the east wing of the Boca Raton Hotel and Club's older section. But things would soon turn sour with the collapse of the 1920s land boom, and by the end of the year, Mizner was back in Palm Beach, deeply in debt.

Some say Mizner's brother Wilson had a lot to do with his plight. Wilson supposedly infuriated T. Coleman Du Pont, one of Mizner's financial backers, by using Du Pont's name in advertisements without authorization, and Du Pont had enough influence with wealthy New Yorkers to make that an expensive miscalculation. However, the architect himself must shoulder much of the blame, according to Raymond B. Vickers. After Du Pont had bailed out of Mizner's dealings, "Addison Mizner participated in a bank fraud conspiracy that financed his extravaganza with depositors' money" to keep from going under, Vickers wrote in *Florida Historical Quarterly*. Mizner and his associates controlled the Palm Beach National Bank and borrowed from the bank more than two hundred percent of its capital, Vickers wrote.

Nothing worked, and in July of 1927, Mizner Development Corporation was declared bankrupt. Four months later, Clarence Geist of Philadelphia bought up the company's properties, including the Cloister Inn. Other than the inn, all that Mizner had built in Boca Raton was the administration building at Palmetto Park Road and Dixie Highway, and twenty-nine modest homes in a subdivision off Palmetto Park Road called Floresta. The largest of the homes was occupied by brother Henry, a clergyman and the only Mizner brother not known as a rogue.

After Mizner returned to Palm Beach, he continued to live in style on Via Mizner, though he was still trying to recoup when he died of a heart attack on February 3, 1933. Singer fared no better. His grand plans to develop the island that bears his name collapsed, and he was arrested on fraud charges in 1927. The charges were thrown out after an eleven-minute hearing in West Palm Beach. He died on June 24, 1932, in London.

The two most important sources for this chapter are *The Many Mizners* by Addison Mizner and *The Legendary Mizners* by Alva Johnston. Other sources include "Joseph Urban's Palm Beach Architecture" by Donald W. Curl; "Palm Beach's Heyday Goes On and On" by Helen Van Hoy Smith; "Addison Mizner: Promoter in Paradise" by Raymond B. Vickers; "Paris Singer Dead" (anonymous article in *The New York Times*); "Palm Beach Architecture Mizner Memories" (anonymous article in *The Palm Beach Post-Times*); and interviews with Mizner scholar Christina Orr-Cahall and onetime Mizner employee Karl Riddle.

Telling Tales on Himself

Brothers Addison and Wilson Mizner probably are the subjects—and the butts—of more stories than any other two Americans who were not presidents. One reason is they started many of the stories themselves, and neither was reluctant to cast himself in a less-than-heroic light if it helped the tale. Addison recorded his memories, up to the death of his mother in 1915, in a book entitled *The Many Mizners.* Some samples:

Mrs. Eyres, a very dear friend of Mother's, had decided to go to Europe for several months, and thought as long as Mama Mizner had such a herd already that it would be nice to leave Bobby with us while she was away. . . .

"Now, my dear children, go out and play nicely with Bobby," said mother.

The great stunt was to ride rapidly down the hill. . . . Bobby begged to have a try at it; of course, we very graciously loaned him the velocipede [bicycle], but neglected to tell him there was a plank over a gully at the bottom of the hill, which, if it was not hit accurately, you broke your neck. Therefore, Mrs. Eyres did not go to Europe, but stayed for a couple of weeks to nurse her child.

Wilson was sent to Santa Clara College, a Catholic school run entirely by priests. The wall about it was 10 feet high. At night they let bull-dogs loose in the yards, which acted as a moat. . . . One night [Wilson] stole a couple of beefsteaks that were meant for the Fathers' dinner and tied them to the dangling rope of the alarm bell.

The dogs were not turned loose until the boys went to bed, and then it took them half an hour to find the meat. . . .

It was Wilson's guilty look that convicted him. He got 10 days on bread and water.

I arrived in Dawson [Yukon Territory] late one night after a two-day trip through muck, mud and mosquitoes, and was dead tired.

I found "Georgie the Moose" [rooming-house proprietress] sobbing in the hall. "I want a bed, Georgie. I'm dog tired."

"There ain't one," she sniffed, "'cept the one Jack Evans and Millie got and God knows when they are going to get them out. . . ."

The door . . . opened . . . and two men were carrying something heavy out, followed by two more doing the same thing. The first load was Jack Evans with half of his head blown off, and the second was Millie. It had been murder and suicide—just a lover's quarrel.

I stopped the sergeant and asked him if the room was vacant, and moved in.

One night I was dining with some social climbers and was surprised to find myself at the hostess' left. . . . She started in by telling me that her daughters had all gone to convents and had become Christians and that they were set.

She shoved a little slip of pink paper under my plate. Thinking it was a love token, I sneaked it under the table and unfolded it. It was a check for two thousand dollars. I passed it back, saying, "You haven't spelled my name right."

What a fool I was in those days.

"Hello, mother. Jiminy, I have been sick for the last 10 days. Never felt worse in my life." He [Wilson] got no further, for mother laughed 'til she cried.

For 40 odd years she had backed up her "Angel Birdie" and now, for the first time, she let us know that she had been on to him all the time.

He hadn't asked her how she felt; just the same old stall and for the first time he hadn't got away with it.

At eight o'clock that night the greatest spirit in the world had slipped away to keep a love tryst with Papa Mizner. ◆

Chapter 20

Arthur Glenn McKee
A Jungle and a Steel Mill

The last of McKee Jungle Gardens almost became a subdivision before a nonprofit land trust rescued it in 1995. In its heyday, it was a corner of the tropics in Indian River County. It also was the least successful thing Arthur Glenn McKee ever did, at least from a financial standpoint.

Sawdust-strewn trails led visitors through dense stands of tropical growth and past ponds festooned with colored water lilies. In all, there were some two thousand floral species, including trees imported from several countries. A biologist once called the 110-acre complex "the finest jungle extant that is at present accessible to the average visitor."

Accessible it was, on U.S. 1 just south of Vero Beach. Successful it was not. Even though twenty-five thousand people a year came during its most popular times, income never covered the money McKee and his partners had plowed into the operation. Extension of I-95 through Indian River County, diverting through traffic from the entrance, was the final indignity. Today, most of the land is developed with homes.

The gardens came about after McKee had reached middle age and had already accomplished a lot by anyone's standards. He was born on January 12, 1871, at State College, Pennsylvania, son of a vice president (later the president) of what today is Pennsylvania State University. After an engineering education at Penn State and fourteen years in various jobs, he decided in 1905 that he wanted to be his own boss. He set up a consulting and contracting company that bears his name and within twenty years was a wealthy man. Arthur G. McKee and Company "designs and builds industrial plants for use in the petroleum, petrochemical, chemical, iron and steel industries," J. Noble Richards wrote in his book *Florida's Hibiscus City, Vero Beach*. "Mr. McKee is credited with many improvements in the production of steel, including blast furnace and the rolling mill operations."

McKee first visited the Vero Beach area in 1922 and soon became interested in the potential of the Riomar section, south of Beachland Boulevard on the narrow island that separates Indian River from the ocean. He probably didn't know it, but Riomar is near the first known settlement in Indian River County: the Ais Indian village of Jece visited by the Dickinson party in 1696. The Ais died out in the eighteenth century, and there seems to have been little Seminole activity in the area in later decades.

The only Second Seminole War installation was Fort Vinton, a stockade thirteen miles southwest of Vero Beach. Some of the settlers who formed the community of Susanna along Indian River under the Armed Occupation Act of 1842 lived near Sebastian River, but most were south of Fort Pierce. After the collapse of Susanna in 1849, when Indians killed one of the settlers, there were rumors that some New Englanders came into the same area in the 1850s, but the next known homesteaders were Gottlob Kroegel and Augustus Park, the latter of whom arrived in 1865, according to *Florida's Historic Indian River County* by Charlotte Lockwood.

In 1874, a post office named New Haven was established, with Thomas New as postmaster, according to the Richards book. A decade later, it was renamed Sebastian. Sebastian was the most important nineteenth-century community in today's Indian River County (created in 1925 after being at various times in St. Johns, Brevard, and St. Lucie Counties), but it wasn't long before there were settlers to the south. By 1890, there were families at Orchid, Roseland, Wabasso, and Vero Beach.

Henry Flagler ushered in the area's modern history when he brought his Florida East Coast Railway through in 1893–1894, giving local settlers reliable, rapid contact with the rest of the nation for the first time. He also established the Gifford community, originally a labor camp for construction crews. About the same time, according to the Richards book, Henry Gifford and Sam Hughes built a ten-foot-wide, unpaved county road (Brevard County) from Fort Pierce to Wabasso for $22.50 a mile. Road transportation didn't mean an immediate boom, however, probably due to the great freeze of February 1895 that destroyed crops throughout the area. At any rate, growth was slow until the Everglades-drainage boom led to the platting of Fellsmere in 1912 and the first plat in what would be Vero in 1913.

Vero, which would be incorporated in 1919, soon became dominant in the area. When McKee arrived, it was still expanding eastward (it would become Vero Beach in 1925), and the post office was taking over delivery to the southern settlements known at various times as Viking, Crawford's Point, and Oslo. He liked what he saw, bought up land in the Riomar area, and began developing it. McKee, though, would have no part of the rampant speculation that characterized the 1920s boom. He sold lots only to people who were planning to build homes. He also built some homes himself and constructed the Riomar golf course and clubhouse, as well as some rental cottages. In 1925, Riomar was annexed to Vero Beach.

McKee's best-known Florida work came about in a roundabout way. Now interested in citrus growing, he was touring the county with Waldo Sexton in search of a grove site one day in 1925 when he spotted the heavily overgrown eighty-acre site that would become his gardens. "As they prepared to clear the land for cultivation," says *The Newsletter of the Garden Conservancy*, "McKee and Sexton were struck by the natural beauty of the site. . . . Instead of planting an orange grove, they decided to plant a garden." McKee wanted to create a thing of beauty and, beyond that, to preserve Florida species that he feared would be wiped out by development. He probably wouldn't have objected to making a little money, also, but he would have to settle for obtaining his other two goals.

"Originally, the acreage was a large Florida hammock," Lockwood said in her book. "The undergrowth was so heavy as to make clearing impractical for the hand methods of the late 1920s and early 1930s, so they left most of it and cut paths through the jungle and spread them with sawdust." McKee, Sexton, and Walter Buckingham had tropical plants collected from all over the world. W. L. Phillips, who later would landscape Fairchild Tropical Gardens in Miami and the Bok Tower grounds near Lake Wales, designed a system of ponds, wetlands, and trails highlighted by a 300-tree Cathedral of Palms.

It took six years to get the grounds ready for visitors. "Ponds were provided with colored water lilies," Lockwood wrote. "More than 2,000 interesting botanical species of plant life were fitted in as if they were growing naturally. They introduced trees from Madagascar, Malaysia, China, South America and Central America without disturbing the charm of the original hammock more than necessary."

Arthur Glenn McKee in his jungle gardens, Vero Beach.
(McKee Botanical Garden)

In the meantime, the land boom had collapsed, and the stock market had tumbled. Nevertheless, McKee Jungle Gardens opened in 1932 and remained a popular attraction throughout the Depression. Though it started as a garden, it soon became what the conservancy newsletter calls "a spectacular jungle experience." McKee and Sexton "populated the garden with an outlandish collection of exotic animals including several species of monkeys, birds and a wrestling brown bear named Doc Doolittle. Then they brought in bathing beauties from all over Florida—including a tiger-striped tunic–clad Tarzanna—to pose among the animals and two giant mushrooms."

Arthur G. McKee and Company also was busy, thanks to Joseph Stalin's determination to make the Soviet Union's industrial base safe from invasion. In 1929, the Soviet government contracted McKee's company to build a huge steel-making center at Magnitogorsk, deep in the Ural Mountains and far from any border. The partnership lasted only three years, due to disagreements between McKee executives and Soviet officials. The McKee firm completed the blast furnaces and the mines, but other companies or Soviet agencies worked on the remaining facets of the complex.

McKee continued to alternate between summers in Cleveland, running his ever-growing business, and winters in Vero Beach, where he tended to his gardens and was a director of one citrus grove and held an interest in another. Now, however, he also made side trips to various parts of the tropical world in search of new specimens for his gardens. He developed a particular interest in orchid culture and set up a special greenhouse in the gardens to house his large collection. He sold orchids throughout the state and furnished royal palms to line Vero Beach streets.

McKee remained active into his ninth decade both in Florida and in Ohio. Though retired from any day-to-day role in his company, he remained chairman of the advisory board. He was a month past his eighty-fifth birthday when he died in Cleveland on February 19, 1956, after a year's illness.

By this time, the era of the superhighway had dawned in Florida. Florida's Turnpike, opened between Dade County and Fort Pierce in 1957, diverted through-traffic from U.S. 1 and hastened the demise of such tourist attractions as the Ancient America mounds in Boca Raton and Waite's Bird Farm in Boynton Beach. When I-95 made its way through Indian River County during the next two decades, the same fate would befall McKee's dream, which had been kept by his family just as he had left it.

"It was either making a carnival out of the place or keeping it natural," McKee's grandson, Arthur McKee Latta, told Peter B. Gallagher of the *St. Petersburg Times*. The gardens never were all that natural, especially not when Doc Doolittle and Tarzanna were on the

McKee Jungle Gardens in the 1970s.
(The Palm Beach Post)

grounds. But, in any case, the McKee family decided to stand still, to some a prescription for failure. "An attraction run just as a gardens can't hardly make it anymore," said Jerome Sheer, owner of Parrot Jungle.

On May 1, 1976, the doors to the McKee Jungle Gardens closed. All but eighteen acres was converted into homes, and the remaining land, the core of the original tourist attraction, was slated for other development until the Indian River Land Trust stepped in. The trust bought the land in 1995 and hopes to have the gardens reopened by the end of 1998.

Sources for this chapter include *Florida's Historic Indian River County* by Charlotte Lockwood; *Florida's Hibiscus City, Vero Beach* by J. Noble Richards; "Natural Beauty No Longer Holds Tourists' Attention" by Peter B. Gallagher; "McKee Jungle Gardens: Reclaiming an American Amazon" (anonymous article); various articles in the Indian River County Library; and an interview with Paul Semon Jr., McKee's son-in-law.

Chapter 21
The Victims of 1928
A Hurricane to Remember

He was born near the dawn of the twentieth century in a sharecropper's shack among the pines of the red-clay country that is northern Florida and southern Georgia. At his birth, he already had two strikes against him: He was African-American, and he was poor. The only thing worse was to be African-American, poor, and female. Monday through Saturday, from dawn to dusk, he labored. On Sundays, he walked down a dusty trail to a crude church—distinguishable from workers' cabins only by its modest steeple—and listened to the preacher assure his flock that the world after this one would be better. Then one day, he heard about a better world that you could reach without dying. It was in the Everglades, along the south shore of Lake Okeechobee, where fortunes were being reaped from the richest black soil anyone ever had seen. By this time, he had reached his early twenties and had a wife and several children, and it took little persuasion to make him head south.

He figured a storm was coming that Sunday in September of 1928, but he didn't realize how bad it would be until it was too late to flee. He and his family huddled in their shack until the savage wind tore it from around them, then struggled blindly through the night toward any haven. They never saw the wave that killed them. Propelled by a northwest wind that battered the frail dike around Lake Okeechobee until it burst, it swept the fields clean of all life, plant and animal.

His body was not found until several days later, so decomposed that those who doused it with gasoline and burned it didn't know who he was or the color of his skin. They knew only that his remains had to be disposed of quickly to avoid the already critical danger of disease. Of an estimated twenty-four hundred people killed in the area of Lake Okeechobee, two-thirds are believed to have been African-American field hands.

Why did it happen? There are several reasons. The first was the right combination of wind and wave pounding a frail dike at the points where the largest concentration of people were hiding. In this case, an inadequate dike was worse than no dike at all; instead of a gradually rising flood, there was a sudden deluge when the dike gave way. Second, communication channels were few; the first highway to the coast was only four years old. Anyway, knowledge of hurricane behavior was rudimentary. And third, many of the homes, particularly the shacks of field workers, were grossly inadequate to withstand hurricane-force winds.

What makes the events of 1928 so tragic is that only two years earlier, two hundred people had been killed on the lake's southwest shore in a similar storm, and nothing had been done to alleviate the danger. Local interests had criticized the state for not using the St. Lucie and Caloosahatchee Canals to lower the water level in the lake before that first disaster. The state had said it was in the business of land reclamation, not flood control.

After the shouting had died down, everyone decided that canal improvements and a larger levee were needed. A twenty-million-dollar bond issue was proposed but promptly tied up by legal action stemming from Dade County. Dade interests said that eighty percent of drainage-district taxes would be levied in that county, but only ten percent of the benefits would be realized there. The upshot was that the bonds were never sold, and the Drainage Board, stripped of funds, virtually had ceased operations by the end of 1927. And that's where matters stood on September 16, 1928.

As in 1926, the summer had been rainy, and once again, the big lake was high. Sunday, September 16th, had dawned cloudy, a bit cool, and windy. Static-filled reports received on the few radios in the Belle Glade area indicated that a hurricane had struck Puerto Rico and caused quite a few deaths but posed no threat to Florida. Some of the people on the low islands at the south end of the lake, concerned about the height of the water and the waves, headed for higher ground outside the dike. But most stayed put; after all, these same islands had come through the 1926 storm just fine.

Residents in the Everglades still may have been in doubt about the storm's path by afternoon, but those on the coast weren't. By two o'clock, the wind had reached gale force at West Palm Beach. By three, a gust of 130 miles per hour had been recorded. And by five, the storm had hit its peak. The winds respected no persons or addresses, though the older neighborhoods generally came through better than did the boom-time developments, most of which had been slapped together with whatever material or labor was at hand during a period when both had been in short supply. In all, twenty-one hundred West Palm Beach families—roughly one-fifth of the population—were left homeless, and property damage was estimated at $13.8 million, according to a file of the Palm Beach County Historical Society. Besides the residences, numerous businesses, industries, and churches were damaged severely. As with Hurricane Andrew in 1992, much of the harm was done when roofs ripped off by the winds left interiors exposed to the ruin of rain.

In Lake Worth, then a city of four thousand, the damage was estimated at four million dollars, and city hall was wrecked. Some seven hundred families were left homeless. Palm Beach reported ten million dollars in damage, but that figure is deceiving due to the extremely high values of the properties involved. In fact, not a single building was destroyed in Palm Beach, and much of the total was attributed to uprooted plantings. Only four fatalities, all in Delray Beach, were reported for coastal Palm Beach County, where a lack of

Wreckage, West Palm Beach, after the 1928 hurricane.
(The Palm Beach Post)

deep floods and waves seem to have combined to keep the toll down. Martin County reported five deaths and four million dollars in damage, mostly to its citrus crops, while Fort Pierce listed $150,000 in damage but no deaths or injuries.

While these coastal residents were digging out, reports began trickling in of deaths in the Everglades. But it would be several days before the outside world would know the extent of death that had occurred below the dike that evening. First to be hit were the islands of Lake Okeechobee. All day long, a north wind had brought water south from the north end of the lake. By evening, the islands had become inundated, and the water was still rising. On Bird Island, twenty-two people took refuge in the Aunapu packing house after their attempts to reach the mainland were frustrated by high water. Ten of them died when the building collapsed under the pressure of wind and wave against a forest of uprooted trees, which had been piled up on the building's windward side. It was 8:20 p.m., and the height of the storm was still to come.

The storm was moving west toward a point on the lake shore north of Canal Point. As a result, the winds along the southeast shore were first from the north, later from the northwest, driving the waves directly into the dike at a spot where population was heaviest. The breaks came about nine o'clock. The first one may have been where the dike ran east-west along the south side of Pelican Bay, south of Pahokee, but no one knows for sure. Within the hour, as many as two thousand would die. A wall of water as high as twenty feet roared across the most fertile—and most densely populated— farmland outside the dike. Field shacks and sturdy farmhouses alike were swept away.

By the time the water reached Belle Glade, several miles from the lake, it was a rolling swell, but closer to the lake it was a pounding hell. South Bay was wiped out. Some two hundred survived by taking refuge on a Huffman Construction Company barge that rode out the storm at its moorings in North New River Canal. An equal number perished. To the east, in the Chosen-Belle Glade area, homes that weren't splintered by the waves were either floated from their foundations or gradually filled with water as those inside first retreated upstairs and then onto roofs, often through holes cut on the spot. Many hung on to survive; many didn't. Before long, a mass of debris that had washed down the Hillsboro Canal from Chosen jammed against the Main Street bridge in Belle Glade. The pressure eventually overcame the latches on the turn span, and the bridge swung open, letting the wreckage through.

Away from the southeast shore, damage was still severe but less so, due mainly to a more fortunate relation of wind direction to levee. South of Pahokee, the south wind following the passage of the eye drove a surge of water from Pelican Bay up Pelican River. Of thirty-four African-Americans who had taken refuge in the barn at Hansen's Dairy, thirty two died. In Bean City, west of South Bay, every house except one was demolished, and at least a dozen people were killed.

An estimated eighty-five people perished in the area between Miami Locks (now Lake Harbor) and Bare Beach, several miles to the west. Clewiston and Moore Haven, which had borne the brunt of the 1926 storm, got off with little damage and no deaths. After a good lashing, the storm cut back across the lake to the land near Okeechobee. Fortunately, this area had neither a heavy population on the shore nor a dike to hold the water back then let it all through at once. Nevertheless, some twenty-five deaths were reported in Okeechobee County.

It would be a couple of days before the road to the coast could be cleared to allow rescue workers in and the dead and homeless out. Within a week, seven thousand refugees had come to West Palm Beach, and more than seven hundred of the dead had been buried there. Some two hundred were buried near Okeechobee and possibly as many as sixteen hundred in the Port Mayaca cemetery under a common marker.

As the days passed, the bodies of the dead became more decomposed and had to be disposed of quickly. On September 26 alone, 267 corpses were burned, 87 of them in a single pyre. Meanwhile, the recovery work continued. Until outside help had arrived, it was supervised by Dr. William Buck, Belle Glade's only physician. But there soon was plenty of help on hand: American Legionnaires, Red Cross workers, National Guardsmen, and others. One pleasant note was the low level of looting. Of course, there wasn't much left to steal.

The second disaster in two years finally generated the pressure necessary to get something done. During the early 1930s, army engineers began replacing the old muck and sand levee with the present structure, which is much larger, made of heavier material, and reinforced with asphalt at vulnerable places. In the process, the shore at Pahokee was straightened and Pelican Bay eliminated; Bacom Point exists today only as the name of a road.

The new dike weathered tests in September of 1947 and again in August of 1949, when hurricanes potentially as deadly as the 1928 storm came through. Though there had been some three hundred thousand dollars in damage to the levee in 1949, it held again. Of course, it never has been tested quite to the extent that its predecessor was in 1928, and there were several areas of seepage when lake levels were high in 1995.

Coming atop the collapse of the land boom, most cities did not fare well in the wake of the great storm. West Palm Beach had a per capita debt of six hundred dollars, which it couldn't pay. Lake Worth was in similar straits. Some boom-time communities, such as Salerno, were disincorporated, while others were cut back in size. Ocean Ridge, for instance, was formed in 1931 from what had been part of Boynton Beach.

When the winds had died down, so had the allure of South Florida living. The latter would not be fully rekindled until after World War II.

Sources for this chapter include *A Cracker History of Okeechobee* by Lawrence E. Will; *Lake Okeechobee* by Alfred Jackson Hanna and Kathryn Abbey Hanna; "The Day Started with Sunshine . . . Then Ended in Horror" by Beryl B. Lewis; the 1956 Hurricane Anniversary Issue of the *Glades County Democrat*; and files of the Palm Beach County Historical Society.

The Rains and Winds of 1926

In 1922, the rains came. In 1924, they returned, wrecking the avocado industry south of Lake Okeechobee and seriously damaging other crops. Fields remained flooded for months; there simply was no place for the water to go. The state's response was to build a low, earthen dike around the southern shore of the lake so future floodwaters would be channeled into the canals. The dike, which ran from Canal Point to about three miles west of Moore Haven, was only five to eight feet high and was not designed for hurricanes; no one had even thought about that.

In any case, the major effort during that period had been completing the St. Lucie Canal between Port Mayaca and Stuart. Virtually everyone believed this was the key to controlling the level of the lake and thus flooding. Still only seventy percent complete, the canal was opened in the fall of 1926. About the same time, a high wind from the southeast brought death to Moore Haven.

The September 18, 1926, storm came inland over Miami and Hollywood on a course toward the northwest. Winds were estimated at 150 miles per hour as the storm roared down on Moore Haven. But as important as the velocity was the direction: Hurricane winds rotate counterclockwise, so the winds lashing Moore Haven as the storm approached from the southeast were coming from the northeast, off the lake. The shallow lake already was high from heavy summer rains. And as the winds rose, it sloshed like a giant saucer of coffee knocked from the side.

At Moore Haven, the water pounded directly against the dike, a structure never designed to take such a beating. And none of the twelve hundred residents was ready. According to Fred Flanders, an engineer in charge of state drainage operations in the area, the only word received was a telegram from the Miami weather bureau on Friday "stating briefly that a hurricane was due to hit the coast in the vicinity of Miami."

By daylight of Saturday the 18th, the hurricane was in full force. "The first break in the dike occurred about three quarters of a mile east of town. This was soon followed by other such breaks. In town the water which had started to come in slowly now began to come in great waves, rising over streets, over floors and then up and still higher," Lawrence Will wrote in his book *Okeechobee Hurricane and the Hoover Dike*. Survivors were carried miles away, hanging to pieces of the wreckage. Many others did not survive.

The eye passed late that afternoon, and the water began to recede. It would be Sunday, however, before the damage could be inspected. And the damage was awesome, even by the standards of 1992's Hurricane Andrew. The *Glades County Democrat* reported that one break in the levee had been sixteen feet deep and that marks on houses indicated the water had been seventeen feet deep in places.

The only other Glades town to feel the brunt of the wind was Clewiston, and that town was protected by a natural sand ridge, not by a weak dike. Flooding was relatively minor, and there were no deaths or injuries, though property damage was extensive in some areas. For instance, twenty of twenty-four homes built by Celotex Corporation were destroyed.

The Moore Haven toll has remained a subject of dispute. The official figure is 150, but those who were there believed it exceeded 200, noting that many victims probably were transients who never had been reported missing. ❧

Chapter 22

The Ashleys
A Legend of the Wild South

Spotting the red lantern, the driver eased his car to a stop at the south end of the wooden bridge over Sebastian River. It was then that he and his companion noticed the heavy chain across the bridge. Another car halted behind them, this one containing four men. As the men in the first car watched, armed men suddenly appeared from the bushes alongside the road and surrounded the second car. Their leader identified himself as Sheriff J. R. Merritt of St. Lucie County and waved the first car through after the chain had been lowered.

What happened next that November night in 1924 remains controversial. Some say it was a shoot-out; others call it an execution. When it was over, the Ashley gang was no more. John Ashley, the leader, was dead. So was his cousin, Hanford Mobley. So were Clarence Middleton and Ray "Shorty" Lynn.

The incident brought to twelve the death toll in a thirteen-year saga of moonshining and jailbreaks, hijackings and shoot-outs, and cast a pall over other members of the family, many of whom felt John had been persecuted unjustly. The Ashley saga may seem small potatoes in an era when battles among drug dealers wipe out more people in a week than the Ashleys killed in a decade, but those times were different.

The best place to begin the tale is December 29, 1911, when a dredge digging the North New River Canal into the Everglades from Fort Lauderdale unearthed the body of DeSoto Tiger, son of Seminole leader Tom Tiger. Jimmy Gopher, a hunting companion of Tiger's, told lawmen that the last person seen with Tiger had been John Ashley. Until then, the Ashleys—father Joe, his wife, and sons John, Bill, Ed, Frank, and Bob—had been just another of the "cracker" families that made up much of the South Florida population in the early days of the century. They were hardworking individualists who cultivated plants, hunted animals, and picked up odd jobs.

Palm Beach County Sheriff George B. Baker dispatched Deputies S. A. Barfield and Bob Hannon to the Gomez area (today in Martin County, then in Palm Beach) to find John. They were walking along Dixie Highway near Hobe Sound when John and his brother Bob came out of the woods with drawn pistols. After disarming the deputies, the Ashleys sent them back south with the admonition: "Tell Baker not to send any more chicken-hearted men with rifles or they are apt to get hurt." Thus was born what would become somewhat of a feud between the Ashley and Baker families.

John stayed out of sight for three years before giving himself up for trial. He was a model prisoner throughout his first trial, which ended in a mistrial, seemingly confident that a jury would not find him guilty of murder—particularly the murder of an Indian—with the evidence at hand. He apparently changed his mind after the state tried to have the second trial moved to Miami, away from those who knew the Ashleys. While being escorted back to his cell by jailer Robert C. Baker (son of the sheriff), he broke away and vaulted a ten-foot fence. He had not been handcuffed because of previous good behavior.

A number of crimes during the next year were blamed on the Ashleys, including a train robbery that went awry when the robbers couldn't agree on what each person was supposed to do. On February 23, 1915, the gang took forty-three hundred dollars from the Stuart bank that now is a restaurant called The Ashley. A stray shot from robber Kid Lowe hit John, costing him the sight in his right eye and forcing him to adopt his trademark eye patch. It also slowed him down enough that a posse led by Sheriff Baker soon ran him down. John was taken to West Palm Beach, then to Miami for the Tiger retrial.

On June 2, Dade County jailer Wilbur Hendrickson answered a knock on his door. The man outside, John's brother Bob, asked him if he were the jailer, then shot him dead before he could reply and took the keys from his body. Obviously, Bob had not thought out

John Ashley.
(Fort Lauderdale Historical Society)

his plan. The commotion caused by the shooting ruined any chance he had of freeing his brother. And there was no driver for the get-away car. Bob leaped onto the running board of a passing delivery truck and ordered driver T. H. Duckett to take him to the "county road." The driver contrived to stall his vehicle just as another truck, carrying Miami policeman Robert Riblett on its running board, caught up. The ensuing shoot-out left both Bob and the officer fatally wounded.

The Tiger case dragged on for more than a year, with tightened security due both to the attempted breakout and to threats from the gang to "shoot up the whole goddamn town" if John were convicted. In November of 1916, though, he pleaded guilty to manslaughter and was sentenced to seventeen years. Once again, he was a model prisoner. In March of 1918, he was transferred from the prison at Raiford to a road camp. Three months later, he and bank robber Tom Maddox fled.

For the next three years, John's activities seem to have centered on moonshining and, with the advent of Prohibition in 1919, rumrunning. John, along with brothers Ed and Frank and Kid Lowe, would race liquor-laden boats from West End in the Bahamas into the maze of waterways south of Stuart along the Intracoastal Waterway. From there, they took the liquor by car to other parts of the state. The business was not without its perils. In June of 1921, John was arrested at Wauchula, east of Bradenton, and returned to Raiford. In October, while bringing in a load of liquor from West End, Ed and Frank disappeared in rough seas.

By this time, the gang had decided it was easier to hijack other rumrunners than to go all the way to the Bahamas for liquor. Under the leadership of Middleton or Roy Matthews, the gang became more feared by the rumrunners than were the beverage agents. Many of the other outlaws paid for protection from the gang's raids. When hijacking fell off in 1923, the gang paid another visit to the Stuart bank. Mobley, a slight and somewhat effeminate teenager, led the raid after entering the bank disguised as a woman. The robbers got away but not for long. Mobley and Middleton were captured in Plant City, Matthews in Georgia.

Capturing gang members proved easier than keeping them in custody. During the next few months, Mobley and Matthews escaped from jail in Fort Lauderdale (the Palm Beach County jail was being remodeled), John broke out of Raiford, and Lynn and Middleton fled a road gang near Marianna. By year's end, the gang had gotten back together in the woods near Gomez.

Bloody 1924 began at Joe Ashley's moonshining camp about two miles from the Ashley home. In February, a posse directed by the younger Baker, who had succeeded his father as sheriff, surrounded the camp. According to the lawmen, a barking dog gave the officers away, and the area soon was a hell of flying bullets. Joe was shot dead as he sat on his bunk, putting on his shoes. Albert Miller, Joe's moonshining partner, and Laura Upthegrove, John's girlfriend, were wounded. "I grabbed my rifle and got behind a forked tree," John told Hix C. Stuart, who wrote *The Notorious Ashley Gang*. "They poured enough lead at me to kill ten men, but fate seemed against them. . . . I noticed a palmetto move, and I let fly a bullet in short order. A man toppled from behind the palmetto and fell prone on his face. I knew I had killed a man. The firing ceased." The dead man was the sheriff's cousin Fred. With his death, the Ashley-Baker feud had become one of blood on both sides.

John took advantage of the lull and fled, but never again would he be far ahead of the law. He was almost caught later that same day, escaping in a harmless exchange of gunfire. Once, at Port Salerno, the gang had to abandon its boat and flee without provisions. Another time, only Mrs. Ashley's warning signal from a window kept John from walking into an ambush near the Gomez home. By October, all the gang's hideouts had been found and destroyed, so John decided it would be a good idea to head for Jacksonville. Somehow, Sheriff Baker learned of the plan. Two of his deputies went to Fort Pierce to alert Sheriff Merritt, who decided to stop the gang at the Sebastian bridge, over which all traffic into Jacksonville had to pass.

Merritt described for journalists what happened on November 1, 1924, when the gang's car appeared. "We waited until they stopped, then came up from behind and covered them with our guns. They were caught unaware, being interested in seeing why the automobile ahead had stopped. When we came up alongside, John Ashley saw me first and grabbed for his rifle. I pushed a shotgun in his face and Deputy Wiggins pushed a gun into his ribs at the same time, telling him to throw up his hands."

After a number of rifles had been taken from the four men, some of the officers left to get handcuffs from their cars, "when Ashley gave a signal and all of the outlaws grabbed for their six-shooters. They had not been searched for them. Right then and there the shooting began, and when the smoke cleared away all four of the desperadoes lay on the ground dead."

That wasn't the only view, however. The men in the first car said that when officers flagged them away from the scene, the outlaws already had been put in handcuffs. The bodies did have marks on the wrists that could have been made by cuffs, but the lawmen insisted the marks happened when the undertaker examined the bodies, and a coroner's jury accepted their version.

A third version, closer to the second than to the first, came to light in Ada Coats Williams' recent book, *Florida's Ashley Gang.* The account, recalled by an unidentified deputy, claims that the gang was in cuffs when John moved forward and started to drop his hands (the deputy didn't say for what reason), which set off the shooting that killed all four.

In any case, Middleton's body was taken to Jacksonville for burial, and the Mobley and Ashley families claimed their own as well as Lynn's remains because there had been no one to speak for him. In the family cemetery next to her home, the mother of the Ashley boys found room for Lynn next to Joe, Bob, John, Mobley, and an infant grandchild—the only one in the group who hadn't died of gunshot wounds.

The killings apparently drove John's girlfriend into a depression from which she never would recover. After a series of arrests for illegal liquor sales and at least one suicide attempt, she killed herself by drinking disinfectant after a heated argument with customers at her Canal Point gasoline station/liquor store.

This chapter is adapted from *The Notorious Ashley Gang* by Hix C. Stuart, with some additional information from "Ten Men Lay Dead Before Ashley Gang Era Ended" by William E. (Bill) McGoun.

Chapter 23

Russell Lynwood Bullard
The Big War Hits Home

For those old enough to remember it, World War II will always be "the war." The nation was completely mobilized as never before or since, and United States combat deaths would total 292,131, more deaths than in any other war the nation had fought and nearly six times the number of victims in Vietnam. Such numbers are numbing, though, because no one can visualize 292,131 people. What can be visualized is the agony of a merchant seaman disfigured by burning oil. During one terrible week in 1942 and virtually in sight of Palm Beach County, seven ships were torpedoed by U-boats. Many victims were brought ashore on anything that would float.

The roughly one hundred thousand residents of Palm Beach County felt fear when German spies were captured near Jacksonville, when they were forced to show identification to cross the Intracoastal Waterway at night, and when they were warned to stay off the beaches because the guard dogs were out. Explosions at sea reminded them why streetlights were shielded so they cast only a small circle of light directly beneath, and why the top half of car headlights were covered to keep light from shining upward—so there would be no light in the sky against which merchant ships would be silhouetted.

Compared to World War II, the Great War of 1914–1918 was hardly more than a skirmish as far as South Florida was concerned. Oh, there were beach patrols in some areas. And ships were required to maintain radio silence and identify themselves by flag when passing the Jupiter Inlet Naval Wireless Station. But there was no enemy action anywhere nearby. World War II was different. People in the area were caught up in the war spirit. They accepted rationing of almost everything with minimum complaint. And they grieved throughout the fighting, as when they heard that Alexander R. "Sandy" Nininger Jr., son of a Lake Worth theater manager, had won the war's first Medal of Honor—posthumously—for heroism in the Philippines less than a month after Pearl Harbor. Or when word was received in July of 1943 that Russ Bullard had become the first Red Cross worker killed in World War II combat.

Russell Lynwood Bullard was handsome, athletic, intelligent, and hard-driving yet personable; in short, he was a winner. In the autumn of 1942, the Lake Worth High School football team he had developed rewarded Bullard's successor, E. R. "Buddy" Goodell, with its first unbeaten year. He symbolized the spirit of the times in that he didn't have to enter into combat but chose to. Physically disqualified from military service, he first took defense work, then joined the Red Cross. He had been away from Lake Worth less than a year when on July 10, 1943, his craft was sunk by Axis bombs during the landing on Sicily that would make the first Western dent in the Fascists' fortress of Europe. Bullard, a native of Georgetown, South Carolina, was just seventeen days past his thirty-fifth birthday when he died.

Russell Lynwood Bullard (far left) and team.
(Museum of the City of Lake Worth)

He had come to Lake Worth in 1937 after six years of teaching and coaching in North Florida. He took over a football team that had won only three of eighteen games the three previous seasons and turned out a winner his first year. His final squad, in 1941, went 7-2-1. As with most successful coaches, Bullard was single-minded while on the job. Mayo Smith, a Lake Worth resident who managed major league baseball teams, remembered Bullard as "a very intense person, somewhat of the Don Shula type" on the field, though "socially, he was great to be around."

The popular view is that World War II came out of the blue, as did the Japanese planes that put much of the United States' Pacific Fleet on the floor of Honolulu's Pearl Harbor on December 7, 1941. In fact, United States' leaders had known for some time the nation would have to get involved sooner or later in the conflict that had broken out in Asia in 1931 and in Europe in 1939. South Florida had become involved, in a way, as early as November of 1939, when a substantial amount of wreckage was found along the beaches of the Jupiter-Hobe Sound area and a six-mile oil slick was observed at sea. The debris apparently came from a German ship that had been destroyed either by storm or by explosion.

On February 21, 1941, Morrison Field (now Palm Beach International Airport) was taken over by the Army Air Corps, which began construction of a major Air Transport Command field, and the county began building the present Lantana airfield to handle civilian traffic. In July, under the guise of a private flight school, a training facility for the Royal Air Force was set up near Clewiston.

Once the United States was officially in the war, facilities were opened rapidly to take advantage of the Florida climate. The handful of residents on Hutchinson Island were relocated to the mainland so the island could be used to practice amphibious landings. Some ten thousand acres of rolling scrubland north of Jupiter became Camp Murphy, site of the army's Southern Signal Corps School. What today is most of Boca Raton between the Florida East Coast and CSX Railroads was made into a giant radar training field for the Army Air Corps. The army also took over the Boca Raton Hotel and Club, and in Palm Beach, the Biltmore Hotel (now a condominium building) became a training center for Coast Guard women and later a hospital. The Breakers was converted into Ream Army Hospital.

Harbor facilities, such as those at Port of Palm Beach and Fort Pierce, were put to military use. The Navy took over airports at Stuart and Vero Beach and used McKee Jungle Gardens for jungle-warfare training. And the army had a small station, Camp Higgins, at Palm Beach Inlet. Out of sight of almost everyone on the coast, prisoners of war were used in the sugarcane fields in camps near Belle Glade and Clewiston.

Convalescing servicemen at the Breakers, Palm Beach, 1944.
(United States Army)

Early in 1942, the war came to South Florida with a vengeance, as Nazi Germany concentrated its submarine forces on the crowded and relatively narrow shipping lanes between Florida and the Bahamas. Germany announced its arrival on February 22 by sinking the *Republic* off Hobe Sound and killing five of the thirty-three crewmen. Three other ships were sunk that month. Besides having a lot of potential targets in a relatively restricted area, the U-boat crews enjoyed a measure of security. Compared to an estimated thirty-four U-boats, the Coast Guard had only thirty-eight ships and forty-three planes in Florida, good odds for attackers whose positions were unknown.

The deadliest week off Palm Beach County began on Monday, May 4. The British tanker *Eclipse* was torpedoed a mile off Boynton Beach. The torpedo came from landward, indicating that the U-boat had lurked within a few hundred yards of shore. The same evening, the cargo vessel *Del Isle* was hit, and two people died. The U-boat forces clearly were not worried about United States' defenses, because while rescue ships still were hovering around the *Eclipse* and *Del Isle*, the tanker *Java Arrow* was torpedoed, and again two crewmen died. The tanker *Lubrafol* was attacked in full view of rescuers at the *Java Arrow*, with thirteen killed.

On Wednesday, the tanker *Amazonas* went down in flames off Jupiter with no survivors, and before dawn Thursday, the tanker *Halsey* was sunk in the same area. On Friday, thirteen of thirty-four crewmen died when the tanker *Ohioan* went down. In all, seven ships had been torpedoed in one week. During that week, Walter "Bud" Cook of Delray Beach alone rescued ninety-nine seamen. Residents and military authorities alike were alarmed.

A new dimension was added to the problem two months later when four German saboteurs were captured shortly after they had been dropped ashore at Ponte Vedre Beach, near Jacksonville. In response, a series of Coast Guard stations were set up along the Florida coast. Mounted patrols rode the beach each night, and attack dogs were used when the terrain would not permit horseback operations. It could be difficult duty for both man and animal. Harry A. Walton of Delray Beach, who commanded the Gulf Stream station, recalled in later years that many of the patrollers were "kids never on a horse before" and that the sand was hard on the mounts.

It was about the time the beach watch was getting under way that Bullard decided he had to do something to aid the effort, even if he couldn't be a soldier. In October of 1942, he was accepted into the Red Cross. After training at Washington, D.C., and at Williamsburg, Virginia, he was assigned to North Africa. By the summer of 1943, the Axis had been beaten in Africa, and the next step was to invade Europe, beginning with Sicily. Bullard, by then a captain in his Red Cross unit, was last seen heading toward the Sicily beach in a landing craft that was under heavy attack by Axis bombers.

Civilians who opted to stay in Florida participated by manning the network of sixty spotter stations set up in towers, some freestanding and others atop existing buildings, such as the old Lake Worth Casino. These military and civilian watchers were tied into a complex of ships, airplanes, and blimps amassed to make southern sea lanes safe for Allied commerce. The nation's first Civil Air Patrol squadron, operating then as now out of Lantana Airport, was one of three groups authorized to look for U-boats on a ninety-day trial basis. It did such a good job—including startling one German commander into running himself momentarily aground—that squadron pilots were authorized to carry hundred-pound bombs.

By the autumn of 1943, the submarine menace had subsided under the relentless pressure of United States forces. Although only three U-boats had been destroyed, the patrols had made it impossible for them to operate effectively. Beach patrols were cut back, and the patrol program finally was dropped in February of 1944, but not before the worst sea tragedy of the war off southeast Florida had occurred, though it was related only indirectly to enemy action. On October 20, 1943, the tanker *Gulf Belle*, northbound with a full load of high-octane gasoline, collided head-on with the empty south-bound tanker *Gulf Land* off Palm Beach. The sea around the two ships became hell. "We couldn't get too close," said Gleason Stambaugh, the Coast Guard officer in charge of rescue operations. "The intense heat singed our hair and curled paint on the boats." Only 28 of the 116 men aboard the two ships survived.

Morrison Field remained a major transportation facility for planes en route to Africa and later Europe. Sometimes, the cargo was quite special. Those in the know realized that when a specially equipped forklift was taken to the flight line, it meant that President Roosevelt was due. The lift would take the crippled president from the plane to rest while the craft was being refueled.

War's end meant celebration, and South Floridians didn't know the half of it. Few of the merrymakers realized that peace would pro-vide the impetus for Florida's biggest boom of all, with thousands of servicemen returning here to live and thousands of others joining them. The celebrants of 1945 were looking back rather than forward. So were the people at Lake Worth High School who dedicated the football field in memory of the coach who had died in far-off Sicily.

Biographical information for this chapter comes from the files of the Palm Beach County school system. Other sources include "Report Russ Bullard Missing" (anonymous article), files of the Palm Beach County Historical Society, and personal remembrances.

Chapter 24

The McCartys
Short, Full Lives

With the hard-fought Democratic primary campaign well behind him and the anticlimactic general election finally out of the way, Governor Daniel Thomas McCarty Jr. was ready to get to work as 1953 began. When he took the oath of office on January 6, he was only forty, the youngest governor in fifty years. And he was the first elected from as far south as Fort Pierce. In fact, he would be the only South Floridian elected governor until Bob Graham of Dade County won in 1978. (Ossian B. Hart, a Reconstruction governor, had been part of the Armed Occupation Act settlement of Susanna on the Indian River, south of Fort Pierce. But he fled after the Indian raid of 1849 and was living in Tallahassee when elected.)

Being entrusted with responsibility at a young age was nothing new for McCarty. His father had died when he was ten, leaving him— the oldest in a household of five children— in charge of family duties. He became Speaker of the Florida House of Representatives at twenty-nine, the youngest person ever in that post, and at thirty-three, he was an army colonel. At forty, he had a lot more ideas.

The keystone of his campaign had been a pledge to block—with a veto if necessary—increases in any tax except the dog-track levy, which he considered to be too low. To that end, he demanded a five percent ceiling on increases for state salaries and expenses. He felt roads should be built on a pay-as-you-go basis and supported the plan of his predecessor, Fuller Warren, for an East Coast turnpike from Miami to Fort Pierce. Among other programs he supported: money and a research laboratory for mosquito control, increased advertising for tourism, more benefits for the aged, and a rebate of gasoline taxes for farmers and commercial fishermen.

On top of the task of setting up his administration and getting these programs under way, the new governor had a heavy social schedule. Together, they were too much. On February 25, less than two months into his administration, he suffered a heart attack. Those who knew him were surprised, even though both his father and his grandfather had died before their fiftieth birthdays due to heart ailments. (His son Michael would die of cancer at age forty-eight in 1995.) He always had been robust, athletically inclined, and a lover of the outdoors. He had played football in high school and softball as an adult. He loved to hunt, fish, camp overnight, and ride horseback through his ranch and groves.

While aides carried on the work at his office, the governor rested. Gradually, his strength began to return. He planned to resume a regular schedule come October 1 and made in early September his first public appearance since the attack, riding several blocks in an open car in the Shriners parade. He caught a cold, and ten days later, he was hospitalized with pneumonia. The additional strain would be too much for his weakened heart. On September 28, Governor McCarty died.

The saga of the McCartys didn't die with the governor; members of the family remain active in public affairs in St. Lucie County. Neither had it begun with him; the family had been there sixty-five years when he took office.

Records are too incomplete to know exactly how many people returned to the St. Lucie County area after the Indian scare of 1849, but a military map of 1856 shows eight families between the present-day cities of Fort Pierce and Stuart. When St. Lucie got a post office in 1868, a steady stream of settlers began joining them. Alexander Bell opened a trading post in 1871; Archibald Hendry and Reuben Carlton, both cattlemen, came a few years later. Another trading post was set up by Benjamin Hogg in 1879, and in 1888, Fort Pierce (then south of the present-day city) got its own post office.

About the same time, a thirty-one-year-old Iowa attorney and educator named Charles Tobin McCarty passed through. "Grandfather came down here to visit on the way to the islands

Charles Tobin McCarty.
(Copyright St. Lucie County
Historical Museum)

with some agricultural project," said John McCarty, the governor's youngest brother and campaign manager, "and he had a freedom from hay fever here and decided to come back."

Just in his early thirties, Charles already had demonstrated the internal drive that would make both him and his descendants stand out. He had completed studies at Tilford Collegiate Academy within a year and after earning a law degree with honors at Iowa State University, had returned to Tilford, where he may have lived out his days had he not learned of the Indian River climate. When he reached Brevard County (as the old St. Lucie County had been renamed in 1855), he became fascinated with the agricultural possibilities and soon was cultivating pineapple and citrus near Indian River, south of Fort Pierce.

He developed a variety of seedless grapefruit that bears his name and became one of the state's largest pineapple growers. In 1895, at the invitation of the British government, he studied the agricultural possibilities of the Bahamas and published his results. Not that he neglected his first profession. At various times, he was attorney for the school board, the town of Fort Pierce, and the Florida East Coast

First soda fountain at Trowell Drug Store in Fort Pierce draws a crowd, circa 1900. (Copyright St. Lucie County Historical Museum)

Railway. He also was a large stockholder in and director of the Bank of Fort Pierce, as well as president of the Fort Pierce Board of Trade and the Florida Horticultural Society. His wife, Barbara Elizabeth, was one of the area's first teachers and, like her husband, was active in civic affairs.

The first major growth in the Fort Pierce area was set off in 1894 by the arrival of the FEC tracks. In 1901, there were enough residents to obtain a charter. Four years later, that portion of Brevard County from Sebastian River south to the St. Lucie River was split off into a new St. Lucie County, with Fort Pierce as the seat.

Charles McCarty would not live long in his new county. On January 30, 1907, just twenty-four days before his fiftieth birthday, he died. Both his citrus and pineapple businesses and his bank directorship passed to his eldest son, Daniel Thomas, born March 31, 1880, in Iowa. All three of Charles' sons also had attended Tilford. While Daniel took over the family businesses, Charles Jr. became a physician in the Midwest, and Brian went into the nursery and real-estate businesses in St. Lucie County.

Daniel McCarty also was the director of two lumber companies, as well as member of a number of civic organizations. In 1920, he became president of what had become the Fort Pierce Bank and Trust Company. Two years later, and less than a month after his forty-second birthday, a heart ailment like the one that had killed his father claimed Daniel.

Daniel's wife, Frances Lardner Moore McCarty of North Carolina, was left to rear five children, the oldest of whom was only ten. Along with staying active in virtually every civic cause, from Red Cross to PTA to church

Daniel Thomas McCarty Sr.
(Peggy McCarty Monahan)

groups, she taught her children to strive for success. They not only strived; they succeeded. All three sons graduated from the University of Florida: Daniel Thomas Jr. in agriculture, Brian Kenelm in business, and John Moore in law.

As soon as Dan McCarty had finished his studies, he took over the family citrus business, but he also had an interest in politics. In 1936, at twenty-four (he was born January 18, 1912), he won the first of three Florida House terms. As a legislator, he sought more money for schools and agriculture, notably for establishing state farmers' markets. He opposed a sales tax, sought a repeal of the poll tax, assisted in the promotion and expansion of unemployment insurance and worker's compensation (the Depression was still on, and unemployment rates were high), and pushed for the abolition of slot machines. In 1941, at twenty-nine, he became Speaker of the House. But as soon as that session ended, he was off on another career.

The nation was mobilizing for the already expected war with the Axis powers, and Dan, who had obtained a reserve commission while at the University of Florida, was called up as a first lieutenant in field artillery. He served in Africa, Italy, France, Germany, and Austria and landed in southern France with the Seventh Army. By war's end, he had become a colonel, and his decorations included the Purple Heart, Bronze Star, Legion of Merit, and Croix de Guerre. His brothers also had reserve commissions and were activated in 1942. Brian was with Merrill's Marauders in the China-Burma-India theater, and John commanded a company in several Pacific campaigns. Each became a major.

After the war, Dan McCarty returned to the family businesses, but his political ambition remained. In 1948, he decided to try for the top, the governor's mansion. He finished a strong second in a nine-man Democratic primary field—Florida was still a one-party state—but lost to Fuller Warren in the runoff. With an aggressive style that was pivotal in the runoff, Warren accused McCarty of being the handpicked candidate of outgoing Governor Millard Caldwell. McCarty insisted he was his own man but declined to mount a counterattack. It just wasn't his style; he was quiet and uncomfortable in crowds, and preferred substantive debate to argument.

In 1952, McCarty was back. And because Warren couldn't run (Florida governors were limited to one term until 1968), he was the front-runner all the way. His chief issue was the economy, but he also was able to exploit what had become the top concern of voters:

morality. Hearings in Miami in 1950 by a United States Senate committee headed by Estes Kefauver, a Democrat from Tennessee, had exposed the extent to which illegal gambling had been condoned and protected by those supposedly enforcing the law. Police Chief Hugh Brown of Boca Raton is one of those who lost his job as a result. Floridians may or may not have been any more moral than when the Bradley casino had been running wide open in Palm Beach, but they did not like the bad publicity. McCarty was in good position to campaign on reform, considering his support of the slot-machine ban and his prominence in St. Andrew's Episcopal Church in Fort Pierce.

Daniel Thomas McCarty Jr.
(Copyright St. Lucie County
Historical Museum)

Opponents Brailey Odham, a Sanford oil man who also stressed reform, and Alto Adams, a Supreme Court justice from Fort Pierce who had stepped down to make the race, attacked McCarty as the handpicked heir of Warren, a potentially damaging charge in light of rumors of corruption in the Warren administration. They also called him a silk-stocking legislator, a machine politician, and a man friendly to the racing interests. This time, McCarty retaliated. He criticized the "desperate charges" made by his opponents and suggested they might be involved in "deals" as well. He almost won a majority in the primary and easily bested Odham in the runoff.

What would have been Governor McCarty's place in Florida history had he lived out his term? Most people seem to think he would have been one of the state's better governors, conservative but constructive and a man of integrity. Despite his illness, most of his legislative programs were enacted, including a two-million-dollar increase in dog-track taxes. Like his father and his grandfather, he knew how to succeed.

This chapter is compiled from files of the St. Lucie County Library and the St. Lucie County Museum, as well as from an interview with John McCarty.

Chapter 25
Zora Neale Hurston
Greatness and Conflict

Today, Zora Neale Hurston is hailed as one of the twentieth century's outstanding authors. Her books are back in print, festivals are held in her honor, and museums, including one in Belle Glade, bear her name. Things were different in 1960. Aside from the hundred or so people—sixteen of them white—who attended her funeral services at Sarah's Memorial Chapel in Fort Pierce, few knew or cared who Hurston had been. She had died a pauper in a Fort Pierce hospital, probably at age sixty-nine, though no one knows for sure. And her grave in the city's old African-American cemetery remained unmarked until 1975, when author Alice Walker had a headstone placed there.

Hurston had been at least three persons: one of the nation's first writers of truly African-American fiction; a collector of African-American folklore in a time when many anthropologists considered African-American culture just a deprived version of white culture; and a focus of controversy. To say that her misfortune was due entirely to her color would be a disservice to the facts. Though it's true she made little from her writings—none of her books sold more than five thousand copies, and her largest royalty check was $953.75—it also is true she often squandered what she did make. Frequently, her earnings would disappear into some improbable scheme, the details of which never would be known.

Yet the feeling persists that if she had been less an "African-American" writer—her subject matter was almost exclusively about the African-American experience—or if she had concentrated on the violence rather than on the sweetness of African-American life, she would have been more successful. As *Saturday Review* once said, "No one has ever reported the speech of Negroes with a more accurate ear." Nevertheless, many readers undoubtedly were and still are discouraged by sentences such as "Dat John is gwine offa dis place effen Ah stay heah."

Her personality was another drawback. She was self-confident, expansive, and assertive in an era when African-Americans were supposed to be self-effacing, reserved, and passive. "Everybody agreed she was quite a character," said Dr. Mildred Hill, who used Hurston's works when she taught black studies and women's studies at the University of Florida. "But that's just about all people agreed upon. She was always surrounded by controversy." Had she lived beyond January 28, 1960, that would not have changed, for she had grave reservations about the great civil-rights movement that had just gotten under way. She felt African-American culture had something to offer that would be destroyed by contact with white culture. In the words of Marjorie Silver, a friend during Hurston's final years, "She wanted to preserve the black race."

In 1960, African-Americans still were a long way from the status they enjoy today. In South Florida, they had the vote and had won the right to use the West Palm Beach Country Club and some beaches. But it would be another eighteen months before the color bar was broken in Palm Beach County schools, and more than another decade before desegregation would be complete. On the other hand, African-Americans were far better off than they had been on January 7, 1891, when Hurston was born near Orlando in Eatonville, Florida, the nation's first all-African-American municipality. At least, that's probably when she was born; she muddied the waters by trying to take a decade off her age.

In those years, African-Americans were on the verge of losing the few gains they had made since the Civil War. Frightened by the near-victory of a biracial populist coalition in the Louisiana state elections of 1896, white Southerners established laws that regulated virtually every phase of African-American activity. In general, African-Americans were not permitted outside of designated areas after dark without written permission. The only place they retained any political power was in communities such as Eatonville, once described by author Theodore Pratt of Delray Beach as "a place of dirt streets, incredibly colorful Negro cabins set beautifully beneath towering live oaks dripping with long beards of Spanish moss."

Hurston might have lived and died in obscurity, as did the poor but proud people about whom she wrote, had not a white woman for whom she had worked as a domestic during her teenage years recognized her talent and arranged for her education. After stints at Morgan Academy (now part of Morgan State University) in Baltimore and Howard University in Washington, D.C., she became the second

African-American to graduate from Barnard College in New York City, and she did graduate work at Columbia under noted anthropologist and social activist Franz Boas. Along the way, she worked at the Library of Congress and was a secretary for Fannie Hurst, a popular novelist of the era. Illustrating the racial climate of the times, Hurst would introduce Hurston as "The Princess Zora" in restaurants where African dignitaries were welcome but African-Americans were not.

Zora Neale Hurston.
(Copyright St. Lucie County Historical Museum)

Hurston's first novel, considered by many to be her best, was *Jonah's Gourd Vine*, published in 1934. It tells of a black Baptist preacher in the Deep South, a man alternately good and sinful. Many saw in Hurston's father, John, a carpenter and preacher, the model for her protagonist. In 1935, she published a book of folk tales, *Mules and Men*. Then for the next two years, she lived in Haiti, studying voodoo rites and producing from this experience a book entitled *Tell My Horse*. Her 1937 novel *Their Eyes Were Watching God* includes a powerful description of the 1928 hurricane in the Glades portion of Palm Beach County. Consider the paragraph from which the title is taken: "The wind came back with triple fury, and put out the light for the last time. They sat in company with the others in other shanties, their eyes straining against crude walls and their souls asking if He meant to measure their puny might against His. They seemed to be staring at the dark, but their eyes were watching God."

In 1939, she retold the Moses story from an African-American perspective in *Moses, Man of the Mountain*. Her autobiography, *Dust Tracks on a Road*, published in 1942, was described by John Chamberlain in *The New York Times* as "saucy, defiant, high-pressure . . . as vivid as a poinsettia, as beautiful as jasmine and as vulgar as a well-liquored fish fry."

During this same era, she also wrote for *The Saturday Evening Post* and for Warner Brothers studio in Hollywood, which could have been especially profitable except for the fact that money had never been a strong motivation for her and she didn't like commercial writing. Besides, she didn't care for the California hills. As she once told Pratt, "I like my land lying down." The tenor of that remark demonstrates her sense of humor, which combined with her love of life and her impetuousness to make her a fascinating, and at times frustrating, person. As Pratt described it:

> She was filled with an effervescence for life seldom seen in the human race. She always had an abrupt, explosive laugh that burst like a bomb. She always had some new idea or project she enthused over. Some she actually carried out. It was both exhilarating and tiring to be with her, for she caught you up in her ideas to the point of exhaustion she herself never seemed to feel.
>
> She was absolutely and completely improvident. Saving what little money she ever earned was a repugnant idea to her. When she did save, it was to pay for some new project, such as an abortive one of mystery involving an expedition to Honduras from which she returned flat broke. I never could find out just what that project was about.
>
> She couldn't help being sensitive of the color line, but her sensitiveness was another kind than usual. It was never bitter. She was always proud of being a Negro and once told me she wouldn't be white for anything in the world.

Yet she was sensitive to the problems her color might cause her white friends. Once, when she was a dinner guest of the Pratts, she stepped out of sight when a white caller came to the door. "She said she didn't want to take any chance of embarrassing us," Pratt wrote later.

Her only postwar book was *Seraph on the Suwannee*, published in 1948. By that time, her creativity apparently was waning. In 1950, she was a maid in Miami, and several years later, she drifted to Fort Pierce and went to work for the *Chronicle*, an African-American weekly she had hoped to make into a nationally known publication. "She ended up doing the makeup, the advertising . . . all of the work," Silver said. "And that just wasn't what she wanted to do."

She began teaching English at Lincoln Park Academy, then the high school for African-Americans in St. Lucie County, but she was fired after a years-old morals charge of unspecified nature was resurrected. "It was a trumped-up charge which was never proven," Silver said. "The other teachers were just jealous of her." She could find little work and could not interest a publisher in *The Life of Herod the Great*, on which she had worked in the small concrete-block house where she lived, constantly delinquent in her rent. "It got to the point that when she had dinner with us, she'd ask to take the leftovers home with her," Silver said. A stroke in 1959 cut off Hurston's work on the Herod book, which she considered her most important piece. She was confined to a nursing home the rest of her days.

Hurston was not an integrationist, yet she believed deeply in developing an understanding between the races. A particularly touching plea is contained in her autobiography: "I give you all my right hand of fellowship and love, and hope for the same from you. In my eyesight you lose nothing by not looking just like me. . . . You who play the zigzag lightning of power over the world, with the grumbling thunder in your wake, think kindly of those who walk in the dust. And you who walk in humble places, think kindly, too, of others. . . . Consider that with tolerance and patience, we godly demons may breed a noble world in a few hundred generations or so."

Sources for this chapter include various letters, articles, and books included in the Theodore Pratt collection at Florida Atlantic University; "Recognition Finally Comes for Black Author" by Mary Jo Tierney; "Zora Neale Hurston: Florida's Forgotten Daughter" by Al Burt; "Zora Neale Hurston, 67, Writer, Is Dead" (obituary); *Their Eyes Were Watching God* and *Moses, Man of the Mountain* by Zora Neale Hurston; files of *The Palm Beach Post*; and personal reminiscences.

The Fight for Civil Rights

From the standpoint of African-Americans, South Florida has changed so much in the second half of the twentieth century that it hardly is in the same world, even considering what some see as backsliding in the 1990s. Today, African-Americans can vote. They attend the same schools as whites, eat at the same lunch counters, patronize the same movie theaters, and play on the same golf courses. They are not bound by law to remain in their neighborhoods after dark. None of that was true at the end of World War II, though the seeds of change had been planted by then.

The total mobilization of the war years opened up job opportunities that African-Americans never before had enjoyed, many of them with the network of military bases that dotted South Florida. But after the war, whites saw the return of peace as a return to the status quo. Though the United States Supreme Court had outlawed the all-white Democratic Party primary in 1944—the primary was all-important in the one-party Solid South—a number of subterfuges effectively denied African-Americans the franchise in nonpartisan local elections.

In West Palm Beach, candidates were picked through a caucus run by a group called the West Palm Beach Citizens Committee. Needless to say, African-Americans were not allowed to vote in the caucus. A 1946 suit to force integration failed, but the committee, seeing that its days were numbered, disbanded the caucus and turned its responsibilities over to the Democratic Party. In 1947, African-Americans voted in city elections for the first time.

The 1954 Brown v. Board of Education decision outlawing public-school segregation had little immediate effect. And nothing happened when the Vanguard Club, an African-American organization that had pushed for voting rights, asked the school board in 1955 to end segregation. It was not until 1961 that five African-Americans would attend all-white Palm Beach County schools; two went to Lake Worth High School and one each attended Seacrest (now Atlantic) High, Jupiter High, and Palm Beach Junior (now Community) College. Full desegregation would take another ten years.

Progress in other fields during the 1950s was moderate and mixed. West Palm Beach's parks and country club were desegregated, but not before it took an eleventh-hour lawsuit to prevent the sale of the golf course and pools to private interests in order to keep them segregated. Delray Beach sold its golf course, retaining the right to buy it back twenty years later, which it did in 1978 under social conditions unforeseen two decades earlier.

Delray Beach nearly had a violent confrontation at its public beach on Sunday, May 20, 1956, when a large group of African-Americans showed up and a crowd of angry whites gathered. Police cleared the beach when the whites began threatening the African-Americans. The city responded the next week with an emergency ordinance banning African-Americans from the beaches and the old city pool at Atlantic Avenue and Ocean Boulevard. The following Sunday, police officers manning roadblocks at all three approaches to the beach confiscated firearms from cars carrying both whites and African-Americans. The ban continued until 1961, when it was repealed and the beach was desegregated without incident.

The 1960s generally were a decade of quiet progress, though there were disturbances in both Fort Pierce and Pahokee over the desegregation of movie theaters. In 1962, attorney F. Malcolm Cunningham won a seat on the Riviera Beach City Council, becoming the first African-American to hold municipal office in Florida in a city with white residents. About that same time, the cause of African-Americans in West Palm Beach was getting a boost that few people recognized. When the Perini interests began developing the area bounded roughly by Clear and Mangonia Lakes, 45th Street, Military Trail, and Okeechobee Boulevard, they started with a subdivision for African-Americans just west of the traditional African-American neighborhood. This was not housing desegregation—that would come later—but it did give African-Americans a chance to own their homes and helped break the grip of land-lords, many of them African-American, who had profited unfairly from the inability of their tenants to find housing elsewhere.

Signs of tension in fully desegregated public schools began to crop up in 1971, when a bomb was found beneath a school bus in Riviera Beach. In October of that year, Boca Raton High School was boy-cotted after sixteen people were hurt in a racial scuffle, and at Lake Worth High, forty-four were arrest-ed in a week of unrest in November. And there were other incidents during the decade.

African-Americans still have a way to go to achieve parity. Official discrimination is a thing of the past, but unofficial and often subtle discrimination continues. African-Americans remain under-repre-sented in professions; they do not get their share of business opportunities; and they have to fight con-stantly to maintain standards in schools with large African-American enrollment. Drugs and crime have taken a terrible toll in older neighborhoods that have lost both their stabilizing middle class to housing opportunities elsewhere and many of their institutions, especially high schools, to desegregation. Hard-won rights seem under continual attack both in the courts and in Congress. Still, few would want to return to the days of Jim Crow and the West Palm Beach Citizens Committee. ❖

Students enter Grove Park Elementary School in Palm Beach
County as full integration arrives, 1970.
(The Palm Beach Post)

Chapter 26
The Fanjuls
An Empire in a New Land

"Why don't you go back where you came from," yelled the Belle Glade pedestrian at a passing car with a New York license plate. He didn't know the half of it. New York was the home of Alfonso "Alfy" Fanjul Jr. in 1960, but just a year before then, his family had fled the Castro revolution in Cuba. They were in the vanguard of a new wave of immigration that within thirty years would change South Florida more than previous waves had changed it in a century.

There had been some immigration from other nations in the early days of the century. Both white "conchs" and African-Americans had crossed the straits from the Bahamas in search of economic opportunities; the Japanese of the Yamato colony near Boca Raton had arrived shortly after the Russo-Japanese War of 1905; and Finns had begun moving into the Lake Worth-Lantana area in large numbers in the 1930s. By and large, however, it had been people from elsewhere in the United States who had put their stamp on South Florida. These immigrants mostly had come from New York and Illinois, Pennsylvania and Ohio, Michigan and Wisconsin, mixing with the farmers already on hand to produce a unique blend of the South, the East, and the Midwest. The balance was more Southern in farm towns—then Boynton Beach and Delray Beach as well as the communities along the south shore of Lake Okeechobee—and more Northern in the West Palm Beach area. Even the Finns often came from the North rather than from Finland directly.

That changed on New Year's Day, 1959, when Fidel Castro marched into Havana to displace the dictatorship of Fulgencio Batista. Batista's brother and his family flew to Palm Beach International Airport that very day. The Fanjuls were not far behind. The leader of the migration was Alfonso Fanjul Sr., head of a financial empire begun by Andres Gomez-Mena, who had come to Cuba from Spain in the 1850s. By the time of the Castro revolution, this empire included ownership or major interests in ten sugar mills, three distilleries, a large rice plantation, cattle operations, major real-estate holdings, and more than three hundred thousand acres of sugarcane land. The holdings had come together in 1936 when Fanjul, born on the island in 1909, married Gomez-Mena's granddaughter, Lillian.

Like many wealthy Latin Americans, Fanjul had been educated in the United States, at Catholic University in Washington, D.C. So when he saw that nationalization of the family holdings was imminent, he fled with his family first to New York City and then to Palm Beach. One story has it that the family smuggled six million dollars' worth of stored sugar out of the country under the nose of a Cuban militia not yet well enough organized to stop such traffic.

The Fanjuls, as did other wealthy Cubans who left soon after Castro took over, assumed Castro soon would fall and they would go back home. It didn't work out that way, so the Fanjuls got back into the sugar business. Osceola Farms, begun with four thousand acres and some old mill equipment, brought in its first crop in 1961: ten thousand pounds. The business steadily grew, and in 1985, the Fanjuls bought the Gulf & Western holdings in Florida and in the Dominican Republic, and became one of the two giants of the Florida sugar industry, rivaled only by pioneer U.S. Sugar.

In 1992, Fanjul-owned companies were producing fifteen percent of the nation's cane sugar, and the family fortune was estimated at more than five hundred million dollars. Later in the 1990s, the Fanjuls opened a refinery at their Okeelanta mill and built new plants to generate electricity from cane wastes. The family also grew in prominence in Palm Beach. The Fanjuls frequently have been listed in the local society pages and have entertained high officials of both the United States and the Dominican Republic governments.

Alfonso Fanjul Sr. would not live to see much of this. He died October 16, 1980, after suffering complications from viral pneumonia. The companies today are run by sons Alfonso Jr., Jose "Pepe", Alexander, and Andres.

Alfonso Fanjul Sr.
(Mort Kaye)

The year of Fanjul's death began a pivotal time for South Florida, though few realized it then. The Mariel boat lift broadened the Cuban exodus by bringing in people generally poorer than previous arrivals, and unrest in Central America sent more refugees north. After conditions worsened dramatically in Haiti later in the 1980s, even more came. Palm Beach County counted 28,505 Hispanics in 1980. By 1990, the number had risen to 66,613, and many believed there had been an undercount in poorer neighborhoods. The largest single group remained Cubans (16,339), but Mexicans (15,228) and Puerto Ricans (12,336) were close behind. The greatest percentage increase was in "other" Hispanics (from 5,489 to 22,680, or 313 percent). Most of these probably were Guatemalans, who have settled in West Palm Beach and Lake Worth in significant numbers, though the list of foreign-born voters alone shows 583 Colombians, 384 Argentineans, 289 Spaniards, 206 Peruvians, 200 Panamanians, and 184 from the Dominican Republic.

There is a large Guatemalan community in Martin County's Indiantown area, and Mexicans have become the largest single minority in Okeechobee County, outnumbering African-Americans. Haitian population numbers are hard to come by, but there may be as many as fifty thousand in Palm Beach County, with major concentrations in West Palm Beach, Lake Worth, Delray Beach, and Belle Glade. The Finnish population is even more difficult to calculate, for Finns are not listed separately in the census. Estimates range from twelve thousand year-round residents to twenty thousand during the winter season, making this one of the world's largest Finnish concentrations outside Finland. The 1990 census also lists 9,116 residents whose roots are in Asia or the Pacific islands and 12,913 others not classified. There are communities of both Koreans and Chinese in the Boca Raton area.

The area is diverse religiously, too. The arrival of Jewish residents from Northern states continued and accelerated in the years following 1960. Many were retirees who moved into such communities as the Century Villages near West Palm Beach and Boca Raton, but many more were younger people with children. The Jewish population in Palm Beach County in 1994 was estimated at 212,000, or 22.6 percent of the county's population, and their vote is significant today in Palm Beach, a town that had been closed to Jewish people in the memory of many old-timers. In the 1990s, Palm Beach County also has become home to an estimated six thousand Muslims, many of them Palestinians in Belle Glade. The county's first mosque was completed in 1996, in suburban West Palm Beach. There are smaller numbers of Hindus and Buddhists.

How have these newcomers been greeted? As seems true of any new arrivals, some have been made welcome, and some have not. The Finns—fair-skinned Northern Europeans—have suffered virtually no discrimination. At the other extreme, Haitians are regarded by many whites as carriers of disease and as drains on the welfare budget and are resented by many African-Americans because they are competition for scarce jobs. Neither stereotype is fair, but perceptions are often what counts.

Sugar harvesting, with cut cane in foreground and smoke rising from field being burned in background to remove leaves.
(The Palm Beach Post)

Despite whatever ethnic battles they have had to fight, the Fanjuls have become the biggest players in an agricultural industry that ranks first among counties east of the Mississippi River. The dollar value of Palm Beach County farming, which was $6.58 million in 1939, hit $1.2 billion in the 1990–1991 growing season. Palm Beach County, in fact, leads the nation in sugarcane and corn value and is third in vegetable value. As of 1987, the county was third in total production, behind two California counties.

Most of the Palm Beach County income is accounted for by the cane fields, which cover more than five hundred thousand acres south of Lake Okeechobee, the vast majority of which is in Palm Beach County. Growers harvested 1.71 million tons of cane in 1992–1993. Despite the encroachment of subdivisions, there also still is a lot of agriculture in the eastern half of the county: $358 million in 1990–1991. Symptomatic of urbanization, the largest single item is nurseries, at $156 million. Vegetables account for $126 million. How much longer that industry will last is an open question.

There is a noticeable tension between other sugar growers and the Fanjuls. It may be due at least in part to the fact that the Fanjuls are immigrants who retain Spanish citizenship, though envy of their wealth and irritation that the family does not live near its farms may also be factors. The fact that the Fanjuls keep to themselves and rarely grant interviews doesn't help.

The Fanjuls and other growers also are targets of environmentalists unhappy about pollution in the Everglades caused by farm runoff; of free-marketeers who dislike federal protections for the sugar industry; and of farm-labor advocates who question whether workers are getting a fair shake—though this last issue has receded in the 1990s after an upgrade in conditions and the use of harvesting machines in place of Caribbean cutters.

Along with the immigrants who remain in South Florida—and most of them are here to stay, regardless of political developments in their homelands—there were others now remembered only in place names: Oslo in Indian River County; Viking (now generally known as Indrio) in St. Lucie County; and Germantown Road in Delray Beach, which was founded by Germans, as its name suggests. Scandinavians were the main settlers of Viking and White City, south of Fort Pierce, in the 1890s.

And there were groups so small or so transient that they barely make the historical accounts. Among these are two groups of settlers who arrived along the south shore of Lake Okeechobee about the time of World War I. One was the colony of Europeans imported by Marian Newhall Horwitz O'Brien to found both Lakeport and the short-lived town of Newhall near Moore Haven. The second was the small colony of Japanese that constituted the first settlement of what today is Clewiston. Not even a name marks their passing.

This chapter is compiled from the files of *The Palm Beach Post*, plus personal reminiscences and an interview with Alfonso Fanjul Jr.

Chapter 27
Davis and MacArthur
Leading the Greatest Boom

At the end of World War II, the coast of southeast Florida was a string of distinct cities, separated in most cases by miles of empty country. Aside from Greenacres and Haverhill, there was little between Military Trail and the Lake Okeechobee communities in Palm Beach County. To the west of U.S. 441, still sometimes called the Range Line, it was open range: a cow could roam free, and the motorist was liable in a collision with that free-roaming bovine. All of that would soon change. The coastal cities would grow together and then spread west, side by side with new cities, and farmland would expand outward from Lake Okeechobee, squeezed out along the coast.

Military installations that had been returned to state or local control were important in the initial stages of South Florida's greatest boom. Bibletown took over much of the Boca Raton air base, and another major portion in the 1960s would become Florida Atlantic University. Morrison Field—again under military control as Palm Beach Air Force Base in the 1950s—became Palm Beach International Airport, with many of the buildings converted to civilian use.

Everything seemed bigger and better than in the 1920s. One reason was the arrival of developers who had become fabulously wealthy in other fields—wealthier by far than any of the 1920s' giants—and were prepared to spend some of that wealth developing on a grand scale. When they bought land, it was frequently by the tens of thousands of acres. When they developed, they developed not just cities but entire areas. Two of these giants moved into Palm Beach County, one at each end, and together set much of the tone for postwar development. In the south, it was Arthur Vining Davis, the person most responsible for the modern aluminum industry. In the north, it was John Donald MacArthur, who became a billionaire largely by selling insurance through newspaper ads at one dollar a pop. Both were the sons of ministers, and both, as is true of most self-made people, were tireless workers. Neither was extroverted, and neither cared much to talk about his money.

Davis was born on May 30, 1867, in Sharon, Massachusetts. After graduating Phi Beta Kappa from Amherst College in 1888, he went to work for Pittsburgh Reduction Company, which had been formed by Charles Hall to produce aluminum by the electrolysis process Hall had invented. Davis' first job involved a bit of everything, as he recalled in later years. "I first worked in the plant—sort of a handyman. Kept mill books, helped in the mill, took an occasional selling trip, nailed up boxes. My starting salary was sixty dollars a month—when I got it." Though it was Hall's genius that brought down the cost of aluminum enough to make

Arthur Vining Davis.
(The Palm Beach Post)

it competitive with other metals for consumer goods, it was Davis' skills as a promoter and salesman that built what in 1892 would become the Aluminum Corporation of America. By the end of World War II, Davis was chairman of Alcoa and had a personal fortune that would reach four hundred million dollars.

With war's end, Davis was among those who were looking to move south. He had wintered in Nassau for some time. But in 1947, he began spending more time in the Miami area, where he ended up building a fifty-acre estate named Journey's End. In 1950, he began to make large-scale land purchases in Dade County. In February 1956, he bought the Boca Raton Hotel and Club and some fifteen hundred acres of land—a mile of which was oceanfront property—from J. Meyer Schine for $22.5 million. The next year, he resigned his Alcoa chairmanship to devote all of his time to his Florida projects.

MacArthur was already on hand. In 1954, he spent $5.5 million for the old Harry Seymour Kelsey property, comprising some twenty-six hundred acres and including most or all of Palm Beach Shores, Lake Park, North Palm Beach, and Palm Beach Gardens. He could well afford it. MacArthur was almost thirty years Davis' junior (he was born on March 6, 1897, in Pittston, Pennsylvania) but by the 1950s he had caught up with Davis financially. In 1928, he started the Marquette Insurance Company with seventy-five hundred dollars in capital, and in 1935, he borrowed twenty-five hundred dollars to take over Bankers Life and Casualty Company.

New tower of Boca Raton Hotel and Club rises behind original Mizner building.
(National Resort Photographers, Boca Raton Hotel and Club - Florida)

Realizing that most people could not afford conventional policies during the depths of the Depression, he hit upon selling through newspaper ads. Even at one dollar a premium, he made money because his overhead was low. Eventually, he would own a dozen hotels, a chain of restaurants, various radio and television stations, twelve insurance companies, utility companies, oil wells, a fabric mill, a bank, a printing company, a car rental firm, a liquor company, and some two hundred thousand acres of land in more than thirty states. His wealth was estimated at as much as three billion dollars.

A comparison of 1950 and 1994 population figures gives some idea of the growth wrought by Davis, MacArthur, and their peers. Palm Beach County's population increased from 114,688 to 937,190; Martin County, from 7,807 to 110,227; St. Lucie County, from 20,180 to 166,803; Indian River County, from 11,872 to 97,415; and Okeechobee County, from 3,454 to 32,325. Once-small cities with ambitious annexation programs grew rapidly. Boca Raton went from 992 people in 1950 to 65,901 in 1994, while Boynton Beach grew from 2,542 to 48,848. West Palm Beach, which was already developed by 1950 with the exception of the Perini holdings, went from 43,162 to 68,703. Lake Worth grew from 11,777 to 29,125; Delray Beach, from 6,312 to 49,298; Belle Glade, from 7,219 to 17,139; Riviera Beach, from 4,065 to 27,259; Stuart, from 2,912 to 13,040; and Fort Pierce, from 13,502 to 36,945. Just as spectacular was the growth of some cities that hadn't even existed in 1950. Port St. Lucie, opened up by General Development Corporation, counted 68,223 people in 1994, while Palm Beach Gardens had 30,046.

At the end of World War II, Palm Beach County had seventeen cities: West Palm Beach (incorporated in 1894), Delray Beach and Palm Beach (1911), Lake Worth (1913), Pahokee (1917), Boynton Beach (1920), Lantana (1921), Riviera Beach (1922), Lake Park (1923), Boca Raton and Jupiter (1925), Greenacres and Gulf Stream (1926), Belle Glade (1928), Manalapan and Ocean Ridge (1931), and Golfview (1937). The postwar rush began slowly with the formation of Glen Ridge and Mangonia Park in 1947 and Highland Beach in 1949. Then the deluge: Haverhill (incorporated in 1950), Cloud Lake and Palm Beach Shores (1951), Juno Beach (1953), Hypoluxo and South Palm Beach (1955), North Palm Beach (1956), and Lake Clarke Shores, Palm Springs, and Tequesta (1957). In 1959 alone, there were six new cities: Atlantis, Golf, Jupiter Inlet Colony, Palm Beach Gardens, Royal Palm Beach, and University Park.

Briny Breezes and South Bay came into existence in 1963. By then, state laws had become tougher to forestall the creation of more "developer cities" with no residents. University Park was absorbed by Boca Raton in 1971, reducing the number of cities in Palm Beach County from thirty-eight to thirty-seven, where it remained until Wellington was incorporated in 1996. The total will again revert to thirty-seven when residents of Golfview sell their land for a Palm Beach International Airport buffer.

In Martin County, where Stuart dates from 1914 and Sewall's Point from 1927, Jupiter Island was incorporated in 1953 and Ocean Breeze Park in 1960. St. Lucie County, which had only Fort Pierce (1901) at the end of the big war, got Port St. Lucie and St. Lucie Village in 1961. In Indian River County, Fellemere (1915), Vero Beach (1919), and Sebastian (1924) were joined by Indian River Shores in 1953 and Orchid in 1965.

In the early years, public reaction to growth was generally euphoric. The old-timers, those who had lived in South Florida before World War II, had lived with a weak job market consisting largely of seasonal work that went to outsiders. During the first decade after the war, little changed, and the job shortage contributed to a "brain drain." College students had to go elsewhere in those pre-FAU days, and many of them stayed away. A breakthrough came when Pratt and Whitney opened its Beeline Highway facility in 1957. Not only did the firm provide a lot of good-paying jobs, it also forced other employers to raise wages to hold on to their workers. The later influx of firms such as IBM, Siemens, and Motorola further improved the situation.

Davis would develop his properties under a corporation named Arvida, which would build extensively in and near Boca Raton. Besides owning more than 125,000 acres in Florida and the Bahamas, he reportedly had two hundred thousand acres on the Isles of Pines that he lost after the Castro revolution in Cuba. His interests were as diverse as MacArthur's: he owned banks, hotels, an ice-cream factory, vegetable farms, a cement plant, a road-building firm, a steel-fabricating plant, a furniture factory, and airline and shipping interests. Davis was nearly ninety when he moved into Palm Beach County in 1956, but he remained active. One of his few concessions to his age was to start eating lunch, on his doctor's orders, after a sick spell in 1960. He moved into a new mansion at Journey's End early in 1962, where the years finally caught up with him. His personal journey ended on November 17.

MacArthur was less reclusive than Davis but more frugal. He would fly tourist class, conduct business from a restaurant table at

John Donald MacArthur in Colonnades coffee shop, Palm Beach Shores.
(The Palm Beach Post)

his Colonnades Hotel in Palm Beach Shores, and collect leftovers after a meal. He knew how to remain in the headlines as his holdings were developed first in North Palm Beach and then in Palm Beach Gardens. In 1961 and again in 1977, he rescued a giant banyan that was to be cut down to make room for development, relocating it in Palm Beach Gardens. He also saved towering palms and Norfolk Island pines. He lured the Professional Golfers Association to Palm Beach Gardens in 1964, then kicked it out in 1973. (It has since returned to different quarters.)

His last major deal was selling the Biltmore Hotel in Palm Beach to Stanley Harte for conversion into condominium apartments. Shortly thereafter, he began to weaken and to lose weight. He was hospitalized at the end of November 1977, and his doctors found inoperable pancreatic cancer a month later. He slipped into a coma on December 29, 1977, and died on January 6, 1978, without regaining consciousness.

During the sixteen years between Davis' and MacArthur's deaths, attitudes about growth began to change. More and more people, especially new residents who had come south in part to escape crowded conditions in the North, began to question the grow-grow-grow psychology. State government responded to these concerns with a series of laws starting with the Environmental Land and Water Act of 1972 and culminating with the Local Government Comprehensive Planning Act of 1985. A key provision of the 1985 law was that local governments could not allow developments unless the public facilities necessary to serve the new people were built at the same time. No longer could city and county officials let subdivisions be built and worry later about how to build roads, police stations, and libraries—at least in theory.

The growth-control movement came to Boca Raton with a vengeance in 1972. By petition and referendum, voters placed in their charter a cap of forty thousand homes. The cap failed court tests, but city councils elected by the same people who had pushed through the referendum achieved the same end through re-zonings and the purchase of oceanfront land for public beaches.

The grow-or-don't-grow issue remained a major concern into the 1990s. Palm Beach County put up one hundred million dollars to buy some of the county's last remaining vacant land. The historic preservation movement was gaining ground, with homes and entire neighborhoods designated for protection. Meanwhile, there was continued pressure to develop the remaining farmland in the eastern part of the county. Proponents of more development argued, as they always have, that growth is good for everyone. Two men who became wealthy selling aluminum and insurance probably would have agreed.

This chapter was compiled from the files of *The Palm Beach Post* and from personal reminiscences.

Bibliography

Alana, Joseph Javier. "Report on the Indians of Southern Florida and Its Keys by Joseph Marina Monaco and Joseph Javier Alana Presented to Governor Juan Francisco de Guemes y Horcasitas, 1760." In *Missions to the Calusa*, edited by John H. Hann. Gainesville, Florida: University of Florida Press, 1991.

Allen, Frederick Lewis. *Only Yesterday*. New York: Harper & Row, 1964.

Amory, Cleveland. "No Run-of-the-Millionaires Here." *The Miami Herald*, March 8, 1963.

Anonymous. Anecdotes about Colonel E. R. Bradley. Personal files of James R. Knott, West Palm Beach, no date.

_____ . "Destruction of Fort Pierce." *The News*, St. Augustine, February 10, 1844.

_____ . "Four Indicted in Everglades Inquiry." *The New York Times*, April 2, 1912.

_____ . *Information for Homeseekers*. Delray Beach, 1913.

_____ . "Richard J. Bolles Dies Suddenly on F.E.C. Train." *Florida Times-Union*, March 26, 1917.

_____ . "Kelsey Gets Millions To Finance Projects." *The Palm Beach Post*, June 14, 1921.

_____ . "H. S. Kelsey Sells 7,458 Feet Along Sea at $350,000." *The Palm Beach Post*, February 17, 1924.

_____ . "Singer Plans Big Beach Resort at Kelsey City." *The Palm Beach Post*, February 19, 1925.

_____ . "Kelsey Buys Florida Canal Co." *The Palm Beach Times*, November 15, 1925.

_____ . "Paris Singer Dead." *The New York Times*, June 25, 1932.

_____ . "Biographies of Prominent Men: Harry Seymour Kelsey." *Palm Beach Sun*, July 9, 1937.

_____ . "Report Russ Bullard Missing." *The Lake Worth Leader*, August 17, 1943.

_____ . "F. Edw. Bryant Dies at Azucar." *The Palm Beach Post*, December 7, 1945.

_____ . "Col. E. R. Bradley, Turf Leader, Dies." *The New York Times*, August 16, 1946.

_____ . "Zora Neale Hurston, 67, Writer, Is Dead." *The New York Times*, February 5, 1960.

_____ . "Palm Beach Architecture Mizner Memories." *The Palm Beach Post-Times*, November 1, 1964.

_____ . "Richard J. Bolles—The Man Behind the Name." *The Bolles Bugle* (Bolles School, Jacksonville, Florida), October 15, 1965.

_____ . *History of Lake Worth*. Manuscript in Lake Worth Public Library, 1970.

_____ . "McKee Jungle Gardens: Reclaiming an American Amazon." *The Newsletter of the Garden Conservancy*, Spring 1996.

Bishop, Jim. *The Murder Trial of Judge Peel*. New York: Simon and Schuster, 1962.

Brink, Lynn, ed. *A History of Riviera Beach, Florida*. Riviera Beach: City of Riviera Beach, 1976.

Bullen, Ripley P. "The Barnhill Mound, Palm Beach County, Florida." *Florida Anthropologist* (1957) 10: 23-36.

Bureau of Economic and Business Research. *Florida Statistical Abstract*. Gainesville, Florida: University Press of Florida, 1995.

Burt, Al. "Zora Neale Hurston: Florida's Forgotten Daughter." *The Miami Herald*, August 22, 1976.

Carter, Ann. "The Intracoastal: Rich in History and Natural Beauty." *The Palm Beach Times*, May 15, 1978.

Clausen, C. J., A. D. Cohen, Cesare Emiliani, J. A. Holman, and J. J. Stipp. "Little Salt Spring, Florida: A Unique Underwater Site." *Science* (1979) 203: 609-614.

Coker, Edward Caleb, and Daniel L. Schafer. "A New Englander on the Indian River Frontier: Caleb Lyndon Brayton and the View from Brayton's Bluff." *Florida Historical Quarterly* (1992) LXX: 305-332.

Cooke, Alistair. *Alistair Cooke's America*. New York: Alfred A. Knopf, 1973.

Covington, James W. "The Indian Scare of 1849." *Tequesta* (1961) XXI: 53-63.

Bibliography

_____. "Billy Bowlegs, Sam Jones, and the Crisis of 1849." *Florida Historical Quarterly* (1990) LXVIII: 299-311.

Cunningham, Thomas M. *The Life and Career of Edward R. Bradley*. Master's thesis, Florida Atlantic University, 1992.

Curl, Donald W. "Joseph Urban's Palm Beach Architecture." *Florida Historical Quarterly* (1993) LXXI: 436-457.

Curry, Pat. "Farming Lures Early Settlers to Boca Raton." *The News*, Boca Raton, October 28, 1984.

Cushman, Joseph D. Jr. "The Indian River Settlement: 1842-1849." *Florida Historical Quarterly* (1964) 43: 21-35.

Day, John A. "Night Watch," Part One. *The Observation Post*, December 15, 1942.

_____ "Night Watch," Part Two. *The Observation Post*, January 15, 1943.

Dickinson, Jonathan. *Jonathan Dickinson's Journal*. Edited by Evangeline Walker Andrews and Charles McLean Andrews. Stuart, Florida: Florida Classics Library, 1981.

Dovell, J. E. "Thomas Elmer Will, Twentieth Century Pioneer." *Tequesta* (1942) VIII: 21-47.

_____. *Florida: Historic, Dramatic, Contemporary*. New York: Lewis Historical Publishing Company, 1952.

DuBois, Bessie Wilson. "Jupiter Lighthouse." *Tequesta* (1960) XX: 5-17.

_____. "Two South Florida Lighthouse Keepers." *Tequesta* (1973) XXXIII: 41-45.

_____. *The History of the Loxahatchee River*. Stuart, Florida: Southeastern Printing Company, 1981.

Farrar, Cecil W., and Margoann Farrar. *Incomparable Delray Beach—Its Early Life and Lore*. Boynton Beach, Florida: Star Publishing Company Incorporated, 1974.

Fernald, Edward A., and Elizabeth D. Purdum, eds. *Atlas of Florida*. Gainesville, Florida: University Press of Florida, 1992.

Fontaneda, Do. d'Escalante. *Memoir of Do. Escalante Fontaneda Respecting Florida*. Miami: University of Miami and Historical Association of South Florida, 1973.

Gallagher, Peter B. "Natural Beauty No Longer Holds Tourists' Attention." *St. Petersburg Times*, July 5, 1976.

Gannon, Michael, ed. *The New History of Florida*. Gainesville, Florida: University Press of Florida, 1996.

Glades County Democrat. Hurricane Anniversary Issue, September 21, 1956.

Glassman, Steve, and Kathryn Lee Seidel, eds. *Zora in Florida*. Orlando: University of Central Florida Press, 1991.

Hann, John H., ed. *Missions to the Calusa*. Gainesville, Florida: University of Florida Press, 1991.

Hanna, Alfred Jackson, and Kathryn Abbey Hanna. *Lake Okeechobee*. Indianapolis: Bobbs-Merrill Company, 1948.

Harner, Charles E. *Florida's Promoters: The Men Who Made It Big*. Tampa: Trend House, 1973.

Henshall, James A. *Camping and Cruising in Florida*. Cincinnati: R. Clarke and Company, 1884.

Hurston, Zora Neale. *Their Eyes Were Watching God*. Chicago: University of Illinois Press, 1978.

_____. *Moses, Man of the Mountain*. Chicago: University of Illinois Press, 1984.

James, Sallie. "Saga of Mollie and the Mercedes To Make Silver Screen." *The Palm Beach Post*, February 21, 1986.

Johnston, Alva. *The Legendary Mizners*. New York: Farrar, Straus and Young, 1953.

Jorgensen, N. W. "The Story of 'Susanna'—First White Settlement in What Is Now St. Lucie County." *News Tribune*, Fort Pierce, April 5, 1972.

Kersey, Harry A. Jr. "The Case of Tom Tiger's Horse: An Early Foray into Indian Rights." *Florida Historical Quarterly* (1975) LIII: 306-318.

Korpan, Steve. "Early Days of Lucerne—Now Lake Worth—Were Exciting, Pioneer Settler Recalls." *The Palm Beach Post-Times*, October 9, 1949.

_____. "'Father' of Kelsey City, Returning After Years, Still Sees Great Lake Park Future." *The Palm Beach Post-Times*, April 2, 1950.

Larson, Lewis H. *Aboriginal Subsistence Technology on the Southeastern Coastal Plain during the Late Prehistoric Period*. Gainesville, Florida: University Presses of Florida, 1980.

Lefevre, Edwin. "Henry Morrison Flagler." *Everybody's Magazine* (1910) XXII: 168–186.

Lewis, Beryl B. "The Day Started with Sunshine . . . Then Ended in Horror." *The Palm Beach Post-Times*, Hurricane Section, September 17, 1978.

Linehan, Mary Collar. *Early Lantana, Her Neighbors—and More*. St. Petersburg, Florida: Byron Kennedy & Company, 1980.

Lockwood, Charlotte. *Florida's Historic Indian River County*. Vero Beach, Florida: MediaTronics Incorporated, 1975.

Lush, W. E. L. "Former Boston Man Sees the Florida City He Started in 1922 'Come to Life'." *The Boston Sunday Globe*, April 16, 1950: 4-A.

Lyon, Eugene. *The Enterprise of Florida*. Gainesville, Florida: University Presses of Florida, 1976.

Mahon, John K. *History of the Second Seminole War*. Gainesville, Florida: University of Florida Press, 1967.

Martin, Sidney Walter. *Florida's Flagler*. Athens, Georgia: University of Georgia Press, 1949.

McGoun, William E. (Bill). "Ten Men Lay Dead Before Ashley Gang Era Ended." *The Miami Herald*, April 14, 1974: 18-BR.

_____. *Prehistoric Peoples of South Florida*. Tuscaloosa: University of Alabama Press, 1993.

Milanich, Jerald T., and Samuel Proctor, eds. *Tacachale: Essays on the Indians of Florida and Southeastern Georgia during the Historic Period*. Gainesville, Florida: University Presses of Florida, 1978.

Miller, Nancy. "Anniversary of Pearl Harbor Recalls Beach Patrols in Area by Coast Guard 'Sailors on Horseback'." *Delray Beach News Journal*, December 9, 1976.

Mizner, Addison. *The Many Mizners*. New York: Sears Publishing Company, 1932.

Moore-Willson, Minnie. *The Seminoles of Florida*. New York: Moffat, Yard and Company, 1911.

Norton, Charles Ledyard. *Handbook of Florida*. 1892

Paige, Emeline K., ed. *History of Martin County*. Hutchinson Island, Florida: The Martin County Historical Society, 1975.

Pierce, Charles William. *Pioneer Life in Southeast Florida*. Coral Gables, Florida: University of Miami Press, 1970.

Pozetta, George E., Ph. D., and Harry A. Kersey Jr., Ph. D. "Yamato Colony: A Japanese Presence in South Florida." *Tequesta* (1976) XXXVI: 66–77.

Theodore Pratt Collection. Various letters, articles, and books at Florida Atlantic University.

Ranson, Robert. *East Coast Florida Memories, 1837 to 1886*. Port Salerno, Florida: Florida Classics Library, 1989.

Richards, J. Noble. *Florida's Hibiscus City, Vero Beach*. Melbourne, Florida: Brevard Graphics Incorporated, 1968.

Rogel, Juan. "Father Juan Rogel to Father Jeronimo Ruiz del Portillo, April 25, 1568." In *Missions to the Calusa*, edited by John H. Hann. Gainesville, Florida: University of Florida Press, 1991.

Rouse, Irving. *A Survey of Indian River Archeology, Florida*. New Haven, Connecticut: Yale University Press, 1951.

Scott, John. *Behind the Urals, An American Worker in Russia's City of Steel*. Indianapolis: Indiana University Press, 1989.

Sears, William H. *Fort Center: An Archaeological Site in the Lake Okeechobee Basin*. Gainesville, Florida: University Presses of Florida, 1982.

Smith, Helen Van Hoy. "Palm Beach's Heyday Goes On and On." *The Miami Herald*, April 26, 1960.

Sprague, John T. *The Origin, Progress, and Conclusion of the Florida War*. Gainesville, Florida: University of Florida Press, 1964.

Stewart, T. D. *A Reexaminaion of the Fossil Human Skeletal Remains from Melbourne, Florida, With Further Data on the Vero Skull*. Washington: Smithsonian Institution, 1946.

Bibliography

Stuart, Hix C. *The Notorious Ashley Gang*. Stuart, Florida: St. Lucie Printing Company, 1928.

Sturtevant, William C. "Spanish-Indian Relations in Southeastern North America." *Ethnohistory* (1962) 9: 41–94.

Sullivan, Robert. "Colossus of Sporting World Holdover from More Spacious Times." *Palm Beach Daily News*, November 4, 1945.

Tebeau, Charlton. *Florida from Indian Trail to Space Age*. Delray Beach, Florida: Southern Publishing Company, 1965.

TenEick, Virginia Elliott. *History of Hollywood*. Hollywood, Florida: City of Hollywood, 1966.

Tierney, Mary Jo. "Recognition Finally Comes for Black Author." *The Palm Beach Post*, May 10, 1978: A1.

_____. "Smuggling Operations Not New." *The Palm Beach Post*, September 3, 1978.

Vallarreal, Francisco de. "Letter of Brother Francisco de Vallarreal to Father Juan Rogel." In "The First Jesuit Mission in Florida." *Historical Records and Studies, United States Catholic Historical Society* (1935) 25: 59–148.

Van Landingham, Kyle S. *Pictorial History of St. Lucie County, 1565-1910*. Fort Pierce, Florida: Sun Bank of St. Lucie County and St. Lucie County Historical Society, 1976.

Vickers, Raymond B. "Addison Mizner: Promoter in Paradise." *Florida Historical Quarterly* (1997) LXXV: 381–407.

Weidling, Philip, and August Burghard. *Checkered Sunshine, the History of Fort Lauderdale*. Gainesville, Florida: University of Florida Press, 1966.

Will, Lawrence E. *A Cracker History of Okeechobee*. Belle Glade, Florida: The Glades Historical Society, 1977.

Williams, Ada Coats. *A Brief History of St. Lucie County*. 1963.

_____. *Florida's Ashley Gang*. Port Salerno, Florida: Florida Classics Library, 1996.

Willoughby, Hugh L. *Across the Everglades*. Port Salerno, Florida: Florida Classics Library, 1992.

Wilson, J. G., and John Fisher, eds. *Appleton's Cyclopedia of American Biography*. New York: Appleton, 1887.

Files of *The Palm Beach Post* contributed extensively to this book, as did the vertical files of various libraries, including those of Palm Beach County, West Palm Beach, Riviera Beach, Lake Worth, Boynton Beach, Delray Beach, Boca Raton, Martin County, St. Lucie County, Okeechobee County, Glades County, Clewiston, Belle Glade, Pahokee, Broward County, Dade County, Florida Atlantic University, and the University of Florida. In addition, anonymous articles in the following newspapers and magazines were used: *The New York Times*, *The Miami Herald*, *Florida Times-Union*, *St. Lucie County Tribune*, *Clewiston News*, *The Bolles Bugle*, and *Fiesta* (magazine). The following museums also contributed materials: the Flagler Museum, the Martin County Historical Society, the Palm Beach County Historical Society, and the St. Lucie County Historical Museum.

Index

Numbers in boldface indicate photographs.

Index

Index

Index

Index